NUMBER SIXTEEN:
The Centennial Series of the Association of Former Students,
Texas A&M University

TEXAS QUILTS, TEXAS WOMEN

TEXAS QUILTS, TEXAS WOMEN

By SUZANNE YABSLEY

TEXAS A&M UNIVERSITY PRESS

College Station

Library of Congress Cataloging in Publication Data

Yabsley, Suzanne, 1949–
    Texas quilts, Texas women.

    (The Centennial series of the Association of Former
Students, Texas A&M University; no. 16)
    Bibliography: p.
    Includes index.
    1. Quilts—Texas—History.   2. Women—Texas—History.
I. Title.   II. Series.
NK9112.Y32   1984   746.9'7'09764   84-40135
ISBN 0-89096-212-X

Manufactured in the United States of America

FIRST EDITION

For Neva Williams

Contents

List of Illustrations

Preface

This is a book about three things—quilts, women, and Texas—and the way they combine to form a unique series of relationships. It is not a how-to-quilt manual; in fact, I have assumed that the reader already knows something about quilts and the way they are made. Nor does the book attempt to make a case for Texas quilts as being superior to, or significantly different from, those made in other places. Rather, my intent is to show how the quilt and its makers have been an integral part of life in Texas since the early 1800s.

The quilt came to Texas with the women of the nineteenth-century westward migrations. It is no exaggeration to state that life in early Texas would not have been the same without the quilt. Everyone from cowboys and dance-hall girls to presidents and first ladies used quilts. And for the women who made them, quilts sometimes became shields against the loneliness and fear that were an inescapable part of their pioneer existence. Today the quilt is still an intimate part of the Texas lifestyle. Its form and uses have been modified, but the importance to its maker is the same.

A quilt is at once simple and complex. Nothing could be more basic than a warm cover. However, the significance of the quilt to its maker carries it far beyond its function into the realms of artistic expression, personal statement, social interaction, and emotional commitment. The quilt has even served as a form of distinctly female communication, as in the post–Civil War story of the circuit preacher's wife told in Ruth Finley's *Old Patchwork Quilts*.[1]

The preacher's wife insisted upon accompanying her husband every time he made his rounds, rather than just once or twice a year as was customary. On the circuit it was standard practice for the preacher to stay in local homes. When only the preacher came to stay it was one thing, but when his wife came with him it was quite another matter, because they were the most socially prominent couple in frontier society. Special housecleaning, baking, and extra preparations were required. One or two times a year the preacher's wife was an agreeable guest; one or two times a month she was an unwanted burden. The overworked women of the circuit finally took action. They let the preacher's wife know that her continual visits were unwelcome by not putting the best quilt on the bed when the pair made their rounds. The message was not lost on the preacher's wife, and she stayed at home thereafter.

Similarly, in a 1917 short story titled "A Jury of Her Peers," a quilt is perceived by women as a means of conveying information among themselves.[2] In the story, a woman has been accused of murdering her husband, but the men who have been assigned the task of gathering evidence find nothing to support the charge. Their wives, however, know the woman is guilty as soon as they see the quilt block she had been piecing. Her stitches, which had been uniformly fine and controlled, suddenly became wildly irregular. It was at this point, they knew, that something had snapped in the woman to make her commit the crime.

In this book, the term *quilting*, which sometimes refers

---

[1] Ruth Finley, *Old Patchwork Quilts and the Women Who Made Them*, pp. 127–28.
[2] Susan Glaspell, "A Jury of Her Peers," in *Literature: Structure, Sound and Sense*, ed. Laurence Perrine, pp. 377–93.

to the entire process of making a quilt, has been used to mean only the actual sewing together of the layers of a quilt: top, batting, and lining. *Piecing* refers to the making of the quilt top, while the term *quiltmaking* represents both piecing and quilting—the entire process.

A great many people have helped me with this project and have contributed to its content. I would like to take this opportunity to thank them all.

I hope that this book will serve as a tribute to the Texas women, past and present, who have expressed their love, care, dreams, memories, hopes, and creativity through the multifaceted medium of the quilt.

TEXAS QUILTS, TEXAS WOMEN

they were just meant as covers
in winters
as weapons
against pounding january winds

but it was just that every morning I awoke to these
october ripened canvases
passed my hand across their cloth faces
and began to wonder how you pieced
all these together
these strips of gentle communion cotton and flannel
      nightgowns
wedding organdies
dime store velvets

how you shaped patterns square and oblong and round
positioned
balanced
then cemented them
with your thread
a steel needle
a thimble

how the thread darted in and out
galloping along the frayed edges, tucking them in
as you did us at night
oh how you stretched and turned and re-arranged
your michigan spring faded curtain pieces
my father's santa fe work shirt
the summer denims, the tweeds of fall

in the evening you sat at your canvas
—our cracked linoleum floor the drawing board
me lounging on your arm
and you staking out the plan:
whether to put the lilac purple of easter against the red
        plaid of winter-going
into-spring
whether to mix a yellow with blue and white and paint the
corpus christi noon when my father held your hand
whether to shape a five-point star from the
somber black silk you wore to grandmother's funeral

you were the river current
carrying the roaring notes
forming them into pictures of a little boy reclining
a swallow flying
you were the caravan master at the reins
driving your threaded needle artillery across the mosaic
        cloth bridges
delivering yourself in separate testimonies.

oh mother you plunged me sobbing and laughing
into our past
into the river crossing at five
into the spinach fields
into the plainview cotton rows
into tuberculosis wards
into braids and muslin dresses
sewn hard and taut to withstand the thrashings of twenty-
        five years

stretched out they lay
armed/ready/shouting/celebrating

knotted with love
the quilts sing on

Teresa Palomo Acosta
Copyright © 1975
Reprinted by permission of the author

CHAPTER 1

The History of Quilts in Texas

Texas Tears, Lone Star, Battle of the Alamo, Texas Republic, Yellow Rose of Texas, Longhorns on the Chisholm Trail, Texas Ranger—the names of these quilt blocks read like a chronicle of the state's history. Since the quilt's introduction into Texas in the early 1800s, it has been a constant and familiar symbol of women's role in the settlement of the state. Abstractions of battles and hardships or colorful events and personalities of the past are rendered on the quilt's surface, but its real meaning is the spirit of its maker.

To look at an early Texas quilt is to see a record of a pioneer woman's life. Its materials grew in her fields and came off her loom or were recycled from clothing worn by her family. The design was chosen because of its particular appeal or significance to her. Perhaps she pieced the quilt alone in a dugout or a log cabin, facing the uncertainty of her existence by being able to control at least the outcome of her own precise seams. She may have quilted it with the help of her family or friends, thus making the quilt a reminder of shared joys and experiences. Perhaps she made it for an anticipated occasion: an engagement, a marriage, a birth, the county fair. Because each step in the quilt's creation was interwoven with the physical and psychological realities of her daily life, a quilt had an emotional component that elevated it far above its function. If a woman's stitches could be translated into words, her quilt would be an intimate, eloquent testimony to her existence. She probably knew that her creation would outlive her, and perhaps that gave her a certain pride, knowing that the quilt, like her, was a survivor.

The pioneer women who came to Texas in the early days faced an intimidating environment. In his book *Lone Star*, T. R. Fehrenbach writes that "vast changes . . . took place in 19th-century Texas. . . . From the first arrival of Anglo settlers in the 1820's through the closing of the final far-west frontier in 1881, life was volatile and dangerous; there was very little security of life or property; the state was always living under some fear or threat. . . . The life was peculiarly destructive of women, eternally the conservators of civilization." Similarly, an old lady of the Texas frontier remarked that the state was "a heaven for men and dogs, but a hell for women and oxen."[1]

Perhaps no single woman's life illustrates the hardships of the Texas pioneer woman better than that of Jane Long, the first of the Anglo women settlers in Texas. The story of Texas quilts and quilters begins with her arrival.

1819–36: Colonization

Jane Wilkinson Long was twenty-one years old when she crossed the Sabine River into Texas in 1819. Against the advice of just about everybody, this remarkable young woman and a teenaged black girl named Kian embarked on a journey unprecedented for females into a decidedly unsettled land.

In 1819 the Spanish territory of Texas was coarse and uncultured. Political intrigue among, and power plays by, various factions and several nations made for a particularly explosive environment. Pirates inhabited the coast. Volatile Comanches watched the alteration of their homeland while Mexico, chafing under Spanish rule, plotted revolution. Ad-

[1] T. R. Fehrenbach, *Lone Star*, pp. 563, 569; Noah Smithwick, *The Evolution of a State, or Recollections of Old Texas Days*, p. 15.

venturers from the United States felt that Texas should ultimately be part of the Union: American privateers cruised the waterways, and filibustering expeditions were the order of the day.

In Texas that year there were few comforts for a woman, and none of the gentler pleasures that had enhanced Jane Long's life before that time. She left behind two babies, her relatives, friends, and familiar social activities in the United States. Ahead in Texas were her husband and the precarious life she had chosen to share with him.

Earlier in 1819 Dr. James Long, leading an American-financed invasionary force, had captured Nacogdoches and declared Texas' independence from Spain. Dr. Long had just been elected head of a provisional government when his determined wife, the first woman of Anglo-American descent known to enter Texas, joined him. Her arrival signaled the beginning of a migration of settlers that would dramatically alter the population and the future of what was to become the twenty-eighth state.

The journey alone would have been enough to make a modern traveler quail; only the most intrepid could have withstood the life that faced her after her arrival. She had to contend with the constant threat of death at the hands of Spanish soldiers, the uncertainty of her husband's military absences, and the death of one of her children. In the middle of winter, only a few days after giving birth to a baby daughter, she single-handedly defended a fort on Point Bolivar from Indian attack. Starvation was an ever-present danger. Finally, she received the dreaded news that her husband, who had been captured and held prisoner in Mexico, was dead. Only three years had passed since Jane Long had entered Texas.

Surprisingly enough, she never lost her love for her adopted home. From the time she arrived until her death, Jane Long was directly involved with many of the most significant personalities and events of Texas history. She knew Jim Bowie, the pirate Jean Laffite, and Colonel Travis of the Alamo. Stephen F. Austin counted her among the members of the "Old Three Hundred," the first immigrant colony in Texas. Two presidents of the Republic of Texas, Sam Houston and Mirabeau B. Lamar, are said to have asked for the widow's hand in marriage.

Because of her close association with the dramatic events and high points of her time, it may seem inconsequential to note that Jane Long was the first woman in Texas who knew how to make quilts. Nevertheless, it is appropriate that a woman whose life was so inseparably linked to the incidents that influenced the early character of Texas should know how to quilt. The quilt, in an unassuming way, is as much a part of Texas lore as are the state's more celebrated symbols.

Jane Long had been taught to quilt by her mother in Maryland as part of the accepted regimen of study for proper young ladies of her day.[2] Maryland's reputation as a center for exquisite quilts goes back almost two centuries. As a daughter of that state, Jane Long received instruction in the art that was assuredly of high caliber. Considering the daunting state of affairs she had to contend with after coming to Texas, it is not hard to imagine Jane Long finding comfort in what few familiar pastimes were available to her; she doubtless took cheer from her needlework.

She pieced quilts, and although there is no documentation to prove that Kian could also quilt, it is reasonable to assume she did. These two women probably spent frightfully lonely evenings together piecing and quilting, and their reminiscences likely made for fascinating conversation over the quilting frames in later years.

The history of quiltmaking in Texas reflects the history

[2]Martha Anne Turner, "Jane Wilkinson Long," in *Women of Texas*, p. 5.

of the settlement of the state. Quiltmaking was not among the forms of needlework practiced by the Mexican, Spanish, and Indian women who lived in Texas when Jane Long arrived. It was not until Anglo-European and black women began to settle in Texas that the art quickly established itself among the different ethnic groups that made up the population.

Ango-European women had brought the ancient skills of patchwork and quilting with them to the New World, and during the colonial period in the United States, those skills were modified and enhanced to such a degree that a distinct needle art form was created. From its very beginnings in North America, the patchwork quilt had an identity and a personality as fresh and exciting as the new land that fostered it. As American pioneers moved west, so did the quilt.

In 1821, after Mexico—and, consequently, Texas—had gained independence from Spain, Mexican authorities granted permission for the establishment of an Anglo-American colony in Texas. Before the close of that year, Stephen F. Austin led the first quota of three hundred families to their new home. This venture was so successful that at the end of the decade the colony numbered more than five thousand inhabitants. Grants for additional colonies were issued to other empresarios, and by 1836, the population of immigrants in Texas had increased to over thirty-five thousand.

1836–45: The Republic

Trouble between the Mexican government and the Anglo colonists was inevitable. Differences in culture, language, and religion naturally caused problems, as did the physical distance between the capital in Mexico City and the colonies. After several years of active colonization, the Mexican

Congress passed a law intended to decrease the numbers of Anglo-American immigrants, increase the Mexican population in Texas, and break up the colonists' flourishing trade with the United States. Amid growing tension, Stephen F. Austin went to Mexico City in 1833 to petition for reforms and was imprisoned there. Ultimately, the Texas colonists revolted against the Mexican government. The battles of the Alamo and San Jacinto were the most famous of the war that established Texas' independence from Mexico in 1836.

The new Republic of Texas, under President Sam Houston, encouraged further colonization using the empresario system. Large land grants were issued. In addition to Anglo- and black-American pioneers, German, French, Dutch, Swiss, Danish, Swedish, Norwegian, and Czech families immigrated in large numbers. Spurred on by the Republic's liberal immigration policy and stories of the "New El Dorado," settlers from more than twenty-five countries were represented in the migration. By the time Texas was annexed in 1845 as the twenty-eighth state, the population had skyrocketed to 150,000. In 1850, the first U.S. census in Texas reported 212,592 citizens.

The relevant factor in this extremely rapid growth was that the immigrants came primarily in family groups. For the first time in its history Texas had a substantial population of women. Quite a few of these women came from cold-weather countries where it was common practice to sleep in feather beds. Because the temperate climate in Texas made feather beds unnecessary, these resourceful seamstresses were not long in discovering a more suitable form of bedding—the quilt.[3]

[3]Mrs. Vincent Kopecky, letter to author, March 12, 1980; Mrs. Milton Brown, letter to author, March, 1980. Some sources, however, suggest that feather beds were widely used in Texas. One story from Parker County in North Texas concerns a woman who escaped an Indian attack by running into the woods. After the Indians were gone she returned to her house to find her

Despite differences in race and culture, the leveling agent of similar circumstances made the exchange of helpful information a common practice among early settlers in Texas. Distance, rather than class distinctions, formed the social barrier in pioneer society. Since the making of quilts was already an established practice in the United States, American women who settled in Texas were only too happy to share their knowledge of such a useful skill with immigrants from other countries and backgrounds. This sharing often took place at a quilting bee.

The quilting bee established itself as one of the main social events in sparsely settled areas of early Texas. In a spirit of mutual support, women would come from miles around to meet at the home of one who had quilt tops ready to be "quilted out." (According to Texas legend, if an unmarried girl completed a patchwork quilt by herself, she would never marry.) The day would be spent sewing and talking over the quilting frames. Men joined the party in the evening for a meal and dancing or singing. Business transactions were discussed, and marriageable young people got an opportunity to look one another over.

An 1834 diary from what is now the Houston area recorded that "the Fourth of July was a fine day. The barbecue was near Mr. Dyer's house, and the quilting and ball were at the house. The ladies spent the day in conversation and work, the young people dancing in the yard, the children playing under the trees, and the men talking politics."[4]

A flowery, yet more detailed, account was written by

---

loved ones dead, furniture and dishes broken and scattered, and her feather beds cut up and emptied of feathers. Her neighbors found her later, in shock from grief, distractedly trying to pick up all of her scattered feathers. See Tressa Turner, "The Human Comedy in Folk Superstitions," in *Straight Texas*, ed. J. Frank Dobie and Mody C. Boatright, p. 201.

[4] "The Reminiscences of Mrs. Dilue Harris," in *Women Tell the Story of the Southwest*, ed. Mattie Lloyd Wooten, p. 243.

one of the male participants at an 1840 quilting bee held in the San Jacinto Bay area. (Spelling and punctuation used are those of the author quoted.)

Not very long after my return from the Sea, there was an entertainment at neighbor Brinsons—an old fashioned country quilting. . . . The quilt was stretched in the primitive way, that is between 4 slats and drawn out to the full size of the quilt— and the 4 corners each suspended by a rope to the cieling—in the best room. Now all the ladies are expected to come early as the Quilt has to be finished before the real fun begins. The Quilters soon take their places—and the work begins on all sides. The gents on the ground are expected to roll up the sides as fast as needed, to pass the thread and scissors—and with anecdotes and small talk to entertain the workers. In the meantime things are getting hot in the Kitchen, the biggest Turkey on the place is basting his back before a huge log fire. . . . The busy hostess flits in and out, now with a word to the needlers and a look of gratified pleasure and pride, and then back to the regime in which all hearts are centered. At last the wonderful quilt is finished—the frames are removed, the Table spread, the Company all in, and joy unconfined rules the hour—but the 3d act is yet in store for us. The shades of night have setteld upon the scene, ere the fragments of the feast are all cleared away—but the sound of the violin expidites further preparations—and now change your partners and "well all dance a reel". . . . At last the morning dawned, the fiddler fled, and after coffee and cake all round, with reluctant partings, the company scattered, and this one event, like all earthly things passed into oblivion.[5]

But the quilting bee was much more than a welcome respite from the pioneer homestead's lonely isolation. It was important in establishing and maintaining the social base as well as the cooperative spirit on which frontier society depended for survival. In addition, the quilting bee was significant in affirming the worth of women's work. Pioneer society was male dominated, and women's influence was,

[5]"Reminiscences of C. C. Cox," *Quarterly of the Texas State Historical Association* 6 (July, 1902–April, 1903): 127–28.

with few exceptions, confined to the family. Warm cover was essential; at quilting bees, women's skills and talents in the production of quilts were publicly recognized and acknowledged.

1845–61: Statehood

The thousands of immigrants who streamed into Texas after annexation in 1845 were driven by dreams of new lives and fresh starts. Resourcefulness and self-sufficiency were the watchwords of the period. Quilts were an indispensable part of day-to-day living at this time, and no frontier household could survive without them.

Making quilts was an activity that "came naturally" in Texas. Materials for their manufacture were as close as the nearest field or the back pasture. Even in the early frontier days, cotton was one of the principal farm crops, and despite the state's justifiable reputation as cattle country, sheep had been a part of the Texas economy since the seventeenth century. Blackjack oaks, sumac, pokeberries, algerita bushes, and numerous other plants yielded dyes to color the homespun cotton or wool.

Aside from quilting frames, which were simply made from any available hardwood, no special equipment was required to make quilts. Each homemaker already had needles, thimbles, and a set of cards for carding cotton or wool. Although cards were primarily used to prepare natural fibers for spinning cloth, the process was basically the same for making batts to fill quilts.

The mechanics of quilting were easily learned. Virtually every pioneer woman, regardless of her homeland or economic status, knew how to sew. Adding the needle techniques of quilting to her repertoire would have been as effortless a matter as a skilled dancer's mastering a simple new step.

The ingenious way in which scraps of precious fabric could be recycled into something useful appealed to the necessarily thrifty side of the frontier woman's nature. The myriad ways those scraps could be combined to form marvelous designs and color combinations endeared the quilt to her beauty-starved senses, and she welcomed the chance to express herself through virtually the only creative medium available to her, needlework.

Life was desperately hard for these pioneeer quilters. The following description of an average homestead in Texas before the Civil War gives an indication of what the environment was like. In such a household, a brightly colored quilt was a warm and cheerful addition indeed.

It was a log cabin, of one room, fourteen feet by fourteen with another small room in a "lean-to" of boards on the windward side. There was no window, but there were three doors, and openings between the logs in all quarters. The door of the "lean-to" was barricaded, but this erection was very open; and as the inner door, from sagging on its wooden hinges, could not be closed at all, the norther had nearly free course through the cabin. A strong fire was roaring in the great chimney at the end of the room. . . . The room was, as I said fourteen feet square, with battens of split boards tacked on between the broader openings of the logs. Above, it was open to the rafters, and in many places the sky could be seen between the shingles of the roof. A rough board box, three feet square, with a shelf in it, contained the crockery-ware of the establishment; another similar box held the store of meal, coffee, sugar, and salt. . . . A canopy-bed filled one quarter of the room; a cradle, four chairs seated with untanned deer-hide, a table, a skillet or bake-kettle, a coffee-kettle, a frying-pan, and a rifle laid across two wooden pegs on the chimney, with a string of patches, powder-horn, pouch, and hunting knife, completed the furniture of the house. . . . A pallet of quilts and blankets was spread for us in the lean-to, just between the two doors.[6]

[6]Frederick L. Olmsted, *A Journey through Texas; or, A Saddle Trip on the Southwestern Frontier*, pp. 99–102.

Hands All Around, ca. 1860; pieced, shell quilting; cotton; 84"x72". By Sarah Pound, Dripping Springs. From the collection of Marguerite Hammack. Photograph by Gary Yabsley.

One older quilter described this pattern as being "like a quilting bee—lots of hands makin' light work." The shell quilting it features is a technique commonly seen on nineteenth- and early twentieth-century Texas quilts.

Odd Fellow, ca. 1860; pieced, shell quilting; cotton; 84"x72". By Sarah Pound, Dripping Springs. From the collection of Marguerite Hammack. Photograph by Gary Yabsley.

This all-over patchwork allowed the efficient use of many different scraps. The aesthetic decisions and the precision required in making a quilt provided pioneer women not only a creative challenge and an economical source of warmth, but also a way to take their minds off their troubles.

Nine-Patch Strip Quilt Top, ca. 1970; pieced; cotton; 86"x72". By Lillian Wren, Wimberley. From the collection of Suzanne Yabsley. Photograph by Jack Puryear.

The Strip Quilt, commonly made of pieces of left-over fabric sewn together more or less randomly, has been a traditional favorite among black quilters. In the center of this quilt is a Nine-Patch, a simple pattern using seams that has always been a popular choice of quiltmakers for introducing a novice to the art.

Women faced a variety of hardships in the young state. Quilting was one of the chief household activities in winter, and in houses that were rather less than cozy, enterprising women found a way to keep their hands warm while working on a quilt. When the cold wind whistled outside, they placed bricks on the floor under the quilt and then set a bucket of hot coals on the bricks. The heat from the coals would rise up and mushroom out, trapped under the quilt. When the quilters' fingers got cold while they worked on top of the quilt, they simply held their hands underneath the frame until they were warm again.

In writing about a cavalry march across Texas, Elizabeth Custer, wife of General George Custer, bemoaned the abundance of rattlesnakes, scorpions, centipedes, tarantulas, seed ticks, and chiggers. She noted, "It was very strange that we all escaped being stung or bitten in the midst of thousands of these poisonous reptiles and insects."[7] These, too, were part of the frontier woman's environment.

Primitive surroundings, inescapable drudgery, threat of Indian attack, disease, predators, and chilling isolation combined to make the Texas pioneer woman's life a daily struggle. Cut off from her past, her relatives, and her friends—with even the nearest neighbor perhaps a day's ride away—she waged a frequent battle with depression.

The young bride from the antebellum South who had met her husband in the lively society of a plantation ballroom faced a far different life when she accompanied him to the desolation of a West Texas ranch. And the European immigrant, perhaps coming from the cosmopolitan environment of an ancient German city, was unprepared for the destructive force of a Panhandle tornado. The farm wife who moved with her family from the settled comfort of New England to start a new life in Texas may have been accustomed

[7]Elizabeth B. Custer, *Tenting on the Plains, or General Custer in Kansas and Texas*, p. 139.

to the hard work of a farmer's existence. But how she must have wished for home the day she looked up from bathing her baby and heard an Indian saying that her child would make "a fine roast."[8]

Mary A. Maverick, supposedly the first American woman to settle in San Antonio, moved to Texas from Alabama. In her memoirs she described the wrenching experience of parting from her family. "December 7th, 1837, we set off for Texas. With heavy hearts we said goodbye to Mother, and my brothers and sister. Mother ran after us for one more embrace. She held me in her arms and wept aloud, and said, 'Oh, Mary, I will never see you again on Earth.' . . . I have never beheld my dear Mother again."[9]

A granddaughter of one of these stoical pioneers recalls their quiet despair.

My grandmother always talked of roses, crimson rambler roses, in Virginia, and she tried all the years of her life [in West Texas] to make a crimson rambler rose grow in her ranch yard. Bluebonnets grew in the pasture, and phlox, and yellow flowers, but nothing ever quite met the need that the crimson rambler rose would have filled in her life. She never complained, and to me, the ranch was a completely beautiful spot. But when I saw mile after mile of real climbing roses on fence rows in Virginia, I realized for the first time in my whole life how the ranch must have really looked to her. She did not tell me that honeysuckle actually covered railroad embankments in Virginia, and somehow I think perhaps she did not dare discuss that, because the nostalgia would have been more than she could bear.[10]

Small wonder that tiny bits of fabric from party dresses and Sunday bonnets, fair ribbons and beaus' neckties were saved and cherished for inclusion in a quilt top. The memories contained in those scraps of cloth were a link to longed-for faces and easier times.

[8] Annie Doom Pickrell, *Pioneer Women in Texas*, p. 23.
[9] Mary A. Maverick, *Memoirs of Mary A. Maverick*, p. 12.
[10] Kate Adele Hill, *Home Builders of West Texas*, pp. xvi–xvii.

There were mitigating factors to counter the hardships, however, and records of the times show that the majority of these women came to love their new homes and instilled in their children a legendary pride bordering on passion for the state. Not the least of the compensations for adversity were the development of self-reliance and the camaraderie shared by the frontier population. A letter written in 1830 by an immigrant from Virginia indicated these aspects of early life in Texas.

Your letter came a month since. I am sure you cannot imagine with what joy it was read; you who receive your mail twice a week, know nothing of the hunger we suffer for news from relatives, friends, and the great world.

But now to answer your numerous questions concerning our Texas home. . . . It was a log house, with two large rooms and a broad hall between; it was considered the palace of the surrounding country. I never remember experiencing a greater thrill of pride than when I stepped into my log castle. Doors were unheard-of luxuries, so I hung gay quilts across the openings where the doors ought to be. A bed and table were my only pieces of furniture. . . . Trunks did for chairs. You may wonder why we do not buy furniture, but when I tell you the nearest town is seventy-five miles away, and that there you must have everything made, you will be not surprised at our condition. Never did I see true hospitality until I came here. Why, at every house, be it ever so humble, you are a welcome guest; they ask you to have coffee or, if it be meal-time, to share their food. The coffee-pot is always kept filled with coffee. I'd like to see you take a drink of it. The average Texan scorns cream and sugar; he wants his coffee as strong and black as possible. I have learned to drink it bitter, for since our sugar gave out we have not been able to get more.[11]

1861–65: The Civil War

Texas had been a state less than twenty years when the Civil War began. The bulk of its citizenry had come from the Old

[11] Anna J. Hardwicke Pennybacker, *A New History of Texas for Schools*, pp. 42, 47.

South and held southern political views. Despite Governor Sam Houston's loyalty to the Union, Texas lined up on the side of the South.

Apparently, a portion of the female population of Texas was not averse to participating in the conflict. A history of women in the West notes that "the western environment produced a number of northern and southern young women who were actually willing to fight beside the men. The *Quincy Whig and Republican* for April 12, 1862, contained a description of an attempt of the Confederate recruiting officers to obtain volunteers at Palo Alto, Texas. Upon noting that but five men responded, fifteen girls stepped forward and declared that they would join those leaving for the front unless their places were taken by men. The article was concluded with the terse statement, "They were."[12]

Texas contributed almost seventy thousand men to the Confederacy, and many of those who did not go to war signed on at home to fight with the Frontier Regiment, a civilian force created by the state legislature in 1861 to defend Texas' embattled western border from Indian attack.

While men were away fighting on one front or another, the burdens on women increased. Accounts of Texas pioneer women list numerous instances of women fending for themselves and their families under hostile conditions. One story tells about a woman who, when her husband was away from home, dressed up in his extra clothing, shouldered a gun, and periodically marched about the property to make the Comanches think she and her children were not alone.[13]

To the endless household duties of women whose men were off fighting were added the responsibilities of procur-

[12] William Forrest Sprague, *Women and the West, a Short Social History*, p. 140.

[13] Pickrell, *Pioneer Women in Texas*, p. 62.

ing food for the family, protecting the homestead against predatory animals and Indian attack, and managing crops and livestock. Bereft of sons, brothers, and husbands and virtually without money, they managed to carry on. Commodities of all sorts became scarce during the Civil War in Texas. The scraps of fabric that could be used in a quilt top were more precious than ever before. According to one source, four yards of calico sold for seventy-five Confederate dollars at this time.[14]

Needlework was so vital a part of everyday frontier life that during the conflict women would band together, stop government wagons, and confiscate cotton from the drivers. A pioneer woman recalled that "on one occasion six hundred pairs of cotton cards were shipped in to Belton [Texas] by some company for sale, and the women just went down and demanded that the cards be given to them as they had to have them and had no money to pay for them. This was done though with grumbling consent."[15]

It is hardly surprising that few masterpiece quilts were created in Texas in this period. A number of quilts made before and shortly after the war years can be found in museums across the state. For the most part, they are not fancy or fine. Their makers had neither the leisure nor the materials to create the intricate works of art that were being produced by their contemporaries in the East. The realities of the situation demanded durable, quickly made covers. Texas quilts that have survived from this period reflect those demands.

And yet there is something in those functional quilts that speaks of spirits refusing to yield to loneliness or grief or fear. It is almost as if the quilt, with its order and preci-

[14] Emanuel Dubbs, *Pioneer Days in the Southwest, 1850–1879*, p. 290.
[15] J. Marvin Hunter, ed., "Reminiscences of Mrs. J. J. Greenwood," *Frontier Times* 2, no. 3 (December, 1924): 12.

sion, was an expression of defiance against the turmoil and confusion its maker faced on a daily basis.

1865–1900: Progress

The Cattle Kingdom

When the Civil War was over, surviving Texas soldiers returned home to a bleak future. One-quarter of the pre-War male population was dead or disabled. The economy was in shambles, property and possessions had been destroyed or scattered, and Confederate money was worthless. Texans were disfranchised. Occupation troops and carpetbaggers moved in.

There was no money. There was no work. No industrial centers existed to provide jobs for the destitute war veterans. In fact, after the Civil War the only things Texas seemed to have more than enough of were open spaces and wild longhorn cattle.

During the war years, longhorns had multiplied rapidly on the unrestricted rangeland. By the end of the conflict, cows outnumbered people in Texas by nine to one. This wily animal proved to be the savior of the postwar Texas economy. The North needed meat, and the abundance of cattle and cowboys in Texas provided the supply. Through a lucky combination of circumstances, ingenuity, and the timely westward extension of the railroad in Kansas, Texans embarked on a twenty-year bovine odyssey that captured the imagination of the world.

The period from approximately 1865 to 1885 marked the great cattle drives of the West. During those years, many thousands of longhorns were herded up two main routes: the Chisholm Trail, reaching from south Texas to Kansas, and the Goodnight-Loving Trail, beginning in the northern part of the state and ending in Wyoming. An entire lifestyle, with its own vocabulary, dress, music, and rules of conduct, developed as a result of these drives.

Part of a cowboy's paraphernalia was the bedroll, which was tied behind his saddle. During a trail drive, the men worked from sixteen to twenty or more hours a day. With so little time for sleep, bedding had to be portable and uncomplicated. The Texas cowboy's bedroll was often a heavy quilt, which he called a suggan. Suggans were made from old wool pants, tailor squares, or the legs of khakis or blue jeans. Apparently, suggans were considered cowboys' quilts only, for they were never used on beds.[16] Some oldtimers relate that the cowboys themselves sometimes helped "tack" their suggans (tacking is a method of fastening the layers of a quilt together by means of single stitches tied at regular intervals), although most of the actual sewing was done by women. A former ranch hand in the Crowell area recalls the general use of this type of quilt and remembers hearing cowboys say, after a hard day's work, "I can't wait to get into them suggans!"

Although it hardly seems possible given the period's powerful hold on the North American psyche, the heyday of the cowboy was extremely brief. Nevertheless, the period and its romance have become a part of our cultural identity. Perhaps not so widely known is the fact that women, too, had an active role in the drama. Margaret Borland of Victoria drove a herd of twenty-five hundred cattle to Wichita, Kansas, in 1873. The only known female trail boss, she took

[16]Mrs. Virgil A. Johnson, letter to author, August 30, 1980. *Webster's Third New International Dictionary* defines *suggan* as an Irish/Gaelic word meaning a coarse blanket used by cowboys and ranchmen; the *Scottish National Dictionary* describes it as a coverlet for a horse's back used instead of a saddle or as a bed cover (information courtesy of Bob Cooper, chaplain, Southern Methodist University, Dallas, Texas).

her seven-year-old daughter and her five-year-old grand-daughter with her on the drive. Several women accompanied their husbands up the trails. Mrs. Charles Goodnight, riding sidesaddle, made the trail drive to Dodge City twice. A spirited businesswoman by the name of Lizzie Johnson drove the Chisholm Trail with her husband on three occasions. Each time she had not only her own herd of cattle but also a separate brand from that of her spouse. Lizzie Johnson was notoriously tightfisted, but she paid six hundred dollars for her husband's casket when he died—an extravagant sum in post–Civil War Texas. It is said that on the undertaker's bill she wrote, "I loved this old buzzard this much." Perhaps most remarkable is the girl who disguised herself as a boy and worked as a cowhand until homesickness caused her to reveal her identity.[17]

Given the customs and demands of the time, it is safe to assert that all of these women owned, used, and knew how to make quilts and that a durable quilt made life more comfortable on their trips up the cattle trails.

A story dating back to 1875 illustrates the quilt's integral role in everyday life at that time. Felix Priddy, a North Texas rancher, was searching Collin County for cattle that had wandered away from his herd. He found his strays among stock belonging to a local farmer, so he stopped, introduced himself to the farmer's wife, and explained the situation. Once his cattle were separated from the others, Felix was invited to spend the night before herding them back to his ranch. While enjoying the farmer's hospitality, Felix learned that in addition to having a houseful of their own offspring, the farmer and his wife had recently taken in two orphaned children. No one seemed to know anything about the little

[17] Emily Jones Shelton, "Lizzie E. Johnson: A Cattle Queen of Texas," *Southwestern Historical Quarterly* 50, no. 3 (January, 1947): 361; Sue Flanagan, *Trailing the Longhorns*, pp. 80–85.

boy of four and his seven-year-old sister other than that their mother had died and their stepfather had deserted them. The boy cried constantly, was afraid of all adults, especially men, and would eat only when the other children brought food to his hiding place in the barn.

When Felix saw this little boy, he was impressed by the child's physical resemblance to members of his wife's family. Margaret Priddy had a sister, Mary, with whom the family had lost all contact; Felix thought that perhaps the little boy and girl might be Mary's children. The following morning he rounded up his cattle and went home, but he returned a few days later with his wife. She, too, noticed the family likeness in the children and asked to see their few belongings. The farmer's wife brought out quilts that the children had carried with them, and there Margaret found the clue to the children's identity. For in the quilts were familiar scraps of her sister Mary's dresses, bonnets, and aprons. Felix and Margaret took their niece and nephew home, and later the children went to live with their grandparents. Doubtless their quilts went too.[18]

Barbwire fences, windmills, and railroads brought about the demise of the open range and the cowboy life. By the 1880s the Indians had been virtually driven out of the state by Texas Rangers, and the buffalo was on the verge of extinction. The face of Texas was changing.

Social Institutions

During this time, the establishment of two social institutions, the fair and the church, encouraged the making of quilts in Texas and notably influenced the quality of their construction. The fair promoted the talents of the individual

[18] Esther Fields Tinsley, unpublished notes on Coe family history (in possession of Betty Peterson, Austin, Texas).

quilter, while the church drew on and advanced the customary communal aspect of the art.

Fairs and expositions provided competition, recognition, and an opportunity to exhibit, all of which were important incentives for the artistic quilter. Before fairs, the only audience a quilter ever had was her family. A rare visitor might prompt the display of a fine quilt on the best bed, but it was not until the fair instituted a special showcase for the presentation of superior talent that quilters had the gratification of reaching a wider public. Quilt contests and the awarding of prizes stimulated a desire for peak accomplishment and broadened the range of expression of each contestant.

Fairs were eagerly awaited annual events in all settled areas. In 1873 the Tenth Annual Fair of Ellis County, held in Waxahachie, offered first prizes of five dollars each for handmade and machine-made "scrap quilts," while the Eighth Annual Capital State Fair, held in Austin in 1882 (with competition "Open to the World"), listed prizes of two and three dollars in several categories of quilt competition.

A premium list from the Third Annual Texas State Fair, held in Houston in 1872, itemizes the prizes that were awarded to the winners in the "quilts and counterpanes" competition.[19] The variety of divisions indicates a keen interest by all ages.

QUILTS AND COUNTERPANES.

Best Silk Patchwork Quilt . . . . Sil. Plat. Cup
Second best Patchwork Quilt . . . . Sil. Nap. Ring
Best White Solid Work, on Muslin . . . . Sil. Plat. Cup
Second best Solid Work, on Muslin . . . . Sil. Nap. Ring
Best Silk Quilt, not before exhibited . . . . Silver Cup
Second best Quilt, not before exhibited. . . . . Sil. Plat. Cup
Best Calico Patchwork Quilt . . . . pair Sil. Nap. Rings

[19] *Premium List of the Third Annual Texas State Fair*, p. 41.

Second best Calico Patchwork Quilt . . . . Sil. Nap. Ring
Best Worsted Quilt . . . . Sil. Plat. Cup
Second best Worsted Quilt . . . . Sil. Nap. Ring
Best Silk Quilt . . . . Sil. Plat. Cup
Second best Silk Quilt . . . . Sil. Nap. Ring
Best Patchwork Quilt, by a Miss
    under 15. . . . . pair Napkin Rings
Second best Patchwork Quilt, by a Miss
    under 15. . . . . Napkin Ring
Best Patchwork Quilt, by a Miss under 12. . Sil. Plat. Cup
Second best Patchwork Quilt, by a Miss
    under 12. . . . . Napkin Ring
Best Patchwork Quilt, by a lady over 50 . . . Gold Spect'les
Best Counterpane, domestic wove . . . pair Sil. Nap. Rings

In 1915, the Texas Woman's Fair, billed as "the first exclusive woman's fair ever held," took place in Houston. Women from seventy counties took part in the fair, which was organized "for the advancement of the interests of women in the entire State of Texas." The Needlework Division of the fair featured three judged classes of quilts: calico, worsted, and novelty.

The first staging of what is now the official State Fair of Texas occurred in Dallas in 1886 and included a quilt contest. Since that time the State Fair has been a focal point for the work of the finest quilters in Texas. The rules for entry have changed little through the years. Each quilt must be the creation of an individual quilter. The promotion of individual artistic achievement has been the chief contribution of fairs and expositions to the art of quiltmaking from their very beginning.

In the last quarter of the nineteenth century, churches emerged as a dominant cultural force on the Texas frontier. Camp meetings and revivals became the main social events of the times in rural areas. The church congregation furnished a peripheral environment suitable to the making of quilts which, like the fair, has continued in existence to the present day. An opportunity to assemble, coupled with the incentive of a common purpose, stimulated quilters to employ their quilting skills jointly for a variety of purposes. Churchwomen honored a favorite preacher with the gift of a special quilt. Members of a congregation who suffered loss of household goods through natural disaster were presented with quilts made by church groups. In many instances, church auxiliary organizations earned money for their congregations' activities through the sale of quilts or quilting services. A newspaper carried a notice in 1888 announcing that "the fine silk quilt donated . . . to the Episcopal Church at this place [Mason, Texas] will be raffled by Mrs. J. M. Lowery. This is the opportunity to make your wife, sister, or your girl a handsome present. $1 a chance."[20] Whatever the occasion, quilters were motivated by a desire to contribute to the work of their religious faiths.

The Last Frontier

The final big wave of immigration into Texas began in the 1870s and continued until 1910. The state legislature, in order to encourage settlement on the western frontier, passed a homestead act and a law exempting two hundred acres of homestead land from debt foreclosure. Most of the immigrants who responded to the offer of land were families escaping from the war-ravaged Southern states, and most of them headed for the arid plains of West Texas and the Panhandle, where homesteads were available.

Their hopeful dreams of a new and better life were frequently thwarted by nature. Drought, wind, dust, and tornados combined to make existence perilous. Because there was no timber from which to make log cabins, sod houses

[20] *Mason News*, December 15, 1888.

and dugouts provided the only available shelter. These crude underground homes had walls and floors of bare dirt, and the only source of light was from the doorway. Centipedes dropped from the sod, and salamanders, tarantulas, and mosquitoes found the dugout a hospitable environment.[21] Again, it was women who had to establish a homelike atmosphere under harsh conditions.

The Wind, a novel written by Texas author Dorothy Scarborough in 1925, relates the tragic story of a young girl who came to West Texas from Virginia during the time of this last influx of immigrants. The book describes the devastating effect of the environment on a woman's mind.

"How did you ever get used to the wind?" [Letty] demanded.

A shrewd look came into the far-seeing old eyes that even yet disdained the use of spectacles. "Honey, that's the hardest thing a woman is up against on the plains. Men don't know what it means to us. Their nerves ain't like ourn. They're made so they can stand some things better nor we can, while agin they're weak as babies about something we don't think enough of to be skeered about." Gran'ma paused a moment, to remember the winds that had harassed her. "I near 'bout fashed myself out over the wind at fust. When I seen my complexion bein' ruint, an' my eyes near 'bout put out with sand, an' my nerves wore to a frazzle, I wanted to holler whenever the wind began to rise."

"That's the way I feel," muttered Letty, her hands involuntarily clenching with nervousness at the thought. . . . "I can stand everything better than I can the wind. The lonesomeness, the lack of anything, the work, nothing's so bad as the wind!"

"Better not think too much about it," cautioned the old woman. "In storm country like this, if I was you, I wouldn't *remind* the Lord of the wind so much!"[22]

[21] Una M. Brooks, "The Influence of the Pioneer Woman toward a Settled Social Life on the Llano Estacado" (M.A. thesis, West Texas State University, 1942), pp. 47, 62.
[22] Dorothy Scarborough, *The Wind*, pp. 194–95.

Although they might have been ineffective against the elements, these courageous pioneer women met the challenges of their new surrounding with astonishing fortitude. The magnificence of their environment, with its spectacular, ever-changing sky and the vast expanses of land, eased the burden of their daily existence. But it was sometimes a quilt that kept them sane.

In *The Quilters*, Mrs. Odessa Wilman recalls her family's life.

I was the oldest child of a family that had settled in West Texas in 1890. My mama was newly married and came from a big, white house in Springfield [Missouri] with elm trees in the front yard and lilacs all around. I don't think she was afraid of anything, but she always said nobody could imagine then what you was getting into out on the plains of Texas. . . . She used to tell how when they come finally to the homestead and the wagon stopped she felt so lonely. There was emptiness as far as the eye could see. How could a human endure?. . . That first summer Mama worked with shovel and pick to build the dugout. . . . Mama said she thanked the Lord that the first dust storm didn't come up till late that summer. She would have turned right around and gone home if she'd seen one first off. . . . Oh Lord. At the horizon the dust came up like a yellow hand between earth and sky and then it kept on rising and rolling toward you till you were right inside it. Small and large twisters and tumbleweeds all mixed up with it and the sand sifted into every pore in your body. . . . She hated being underground but she said at least you didn't hear the wind so loud. The sand would sift in through the door until you felt buried alive. . . . The first time Mama was left alone was when Papa hitched up the wagon to go after firewood. . . . That was late September. Mama had her garden in and she was plowing more land for corn when the first dust storm came up. The wind blew for three days so hard and the air was so full of dust that she had to tie a rope around her waist to get out to feed and milk the cow. There was nothing else but to endure it. She had never heard sounds like was in the wind. She took to quilting all day every day. She used to say, "If I hadn't had the piecing, I don't know what I would have done." There was nobody to talk to and no where to go to get away from the wind except underground. She got to worrying about freezing to death in the winter. She used to laugh when she told it, how you never saw anyone quilt so fast in your life. Mama's best quilts were her dugout quilts because that was when she really needed something pretty. She made a Butterfly and a Dresden Plate and a Flower Basket during those two years in the dugout. After a while she got to like the sound of the wind, if it didn't go on too long, and she could get real soothed with that sound and the needlework at night sitting by the lamp. She made the Basket for Papa. She started the Butterfly in that first dust storm all alone. . . . The Butterfly was free and fragile. It was the prettiest thing she could think of. She knew I was coming along and the Butterfly was for me.[23]

A minor regional quilting variation may have its roots in those early days of dugout living. In the Panhandle, the traditional manner of quilting is slightly different from that found in central Texas. In the Hill Country, quilting is commonly done "in the ditch," that is, in the seams of the pieced pattern. Old-time Panhandle quilters, however, quilt on both sides of a seam. Whereas central Texas needlewomen might regard this practice as a waste of thread, to the Panhandle quilter, staying out of a "ditch" might have a symbolic significance dating back to harder times.

1900–30: A New Century

Because of its violent and tumultuous history of settlement, Texas entered the twentieth century several decades behind the rest of the United States in social and industrial development. Its immense land area kept its citizens remote not

[23] Patricia Cooper and Norma Bradley Buferd, *The Quilters*, pp. 21–24.

only from each other but from the rest of the country as well. A rural state with relatively few cities, Texas was outside the mainstream of popular culture. Nevertheless, fashion trends and the widespread influence of Victorian styles were evident in the more established areas of the state.

Women whose homesteading days were behind them and those of the second generation of settled pioneer families had more leisure time as well as the means with which to indulge themselves. It was during this period, roughly from 1880 to 1900, that the Victorian crazy quilt and the slumber or parlor throw came into vogue.

In the strictest sense,they are not actually quilts, because they often have no batting and are usually tacked rather than quilted to their linings. They are primarily freeform showcases for prized pieces of fine fabric and for displaying the embroidery skills of their makers. But because patchwork is an essential element in their construction,the crazy quilt and the slumber throw can be classsed as variations of the quilt.

San Antonio and Dallas appear to have been centers for this type of needle art in Texas. Crazy quilts won the Textiles Division of San Antonio's International Exposition and the Dallas State Fair's quilt contest for several years running around the turn of the century.

In the early 1900s, while much of the rest of the country enjoyed store-bought mass-produced covers, the people of rural Texas still used the homemade quilt as the chief means of warmth. Young women were taught to quilt by their mothers and grandmothers and were expected to do their share in making bedclothes for the family. Many present-day Texas quilters recall learning to quilt as a required part of their childhood lessons. Wilna Morton Daugherty, whose family settled on a ranch north of Amarillo in 1902, vividly remembers the process.

Dutch Doll, 1932, and String Sampler, 1939; Dutch Doll, cotton, 72"x-60"; String Sampler, cotton, 84"x72". By Hattie Mae Coffee, Payton Colony. From the collection of the artist.

The Dutch Doll Quilt shown here is a fine testament to the intergenerational value of quilting; begun by Melissa Jones, it was finished by her daughter, Hattie Mae Coffee. The String Quilt is similar to the Strip Quilt but uses narrower pieces of fabric. Some students of folk art believe the vibrant colors typical of quilts made by black women show the influence of African needle arts.

Appliquéd and embroidered quilt, 1980; cotton. By Virginia Quintanilla, San Antonio. In the collection of the artist.

Choices of color and technique may both reflect cultural influences. The appliqué work on this brilliantly colored quilt is reminiscent of the *colchas bordadas* of Mexican needle work.

Lone Star, ca. 1930; pieced; cotton; 106"x92". Star pieced by Lila Dorsey Moore, Orange. Design and setting by Gail Lane, Bastrop. From the collection of Gail Lane. Photograph by Greg White, courtesy of *Texas Highways* magazine.

The quilting designs, which show the artistic adaptation of cultural influences, were taken from rubbings of grave stones in Bastrop County. The quilting itself was done by the Sunday Friends, Austin.

Star Flower, 1980; pieced wall hanging; cotton; 42" octagon. Designed and quilted by Connie Hufnagel, Austin. In the collection of the artist.

This quilted work illustrates how the traditional craft has been recog-nized and developed as an art form by contemporary women. Connie Hufnagel, whose original quilt designs have won numerous awards, is becoming nationally known for her work.

Texas Star, ca. 1850; pieced; silk, satin, and taffeta; 83"x72½". By Jane Morley, Marshall. From the collection of the San Antonio Museum Association, by permission.

Mrs. Morley was born in England and immigrated to Texas in the 1840s or 1850s. Family history relates that she chose a Lone Star pattern for her quilt's central motif because she was so proud of her adopted state. The colors of this quilt are red, white, and blue.

Ocean Waves, 1877; pieced; calico, gingham, muslin, and homespun; 95"x72". By Matilda Jane Sanford, Shelby County. From the collection of the San Antonio Museum Association, by permission.

This quilt, in a popular pattern of the day, illustrates the close involvement of the pioneer quilter with her creation. The cotton for the lining of this cover was grown on the Sanford farm in East Texas and was carded, spun, and woven by Mrs. Sanford. The quilt top contains calico purchased in Shreveport, Louisiana, and the pieces used were almost certainly from carefully saved remnants or recycled portions of family garments made of the prized fabric. Mrs. Sanford made the quilt in anticipation of the birth of her second child.

Postage Stamp Quilt in Quilt Chest. From the collection of the Rusk County Heritage Association, Henderson. Photograph by Katie Lee Hunt.

This quilt chest was built in 1804, of pine, with handwrought hinges, by Willis Goodlett, who brought it to Texas in 1859. The coverlet (1813) on its lid is a white, handwoven counterpane, embroidered and bordered with a hand-knotted fringe. The quilt dates from around the middle of the nineteenth century and was given to the Heritage Association by Mrs. Josie Moore of Arp.

Suggan, ca. 1900; pieced and tacked; wool tailor samples; 90"x72". By Mrs. P. P. Cooper, Crowell. From the collection of the Fire Hall Museum, Crowell. Photograph by David Polasek.

Quilts have been an important part of the westward movement in our country and, naturally enough, had a role to play in the life of the range cowboy as well as the homesteader. The suggan is a simple version of a quilt, with the emphasis definitely on function rather than form.

Mrs. Morton taught her girls the things that a woman should be able to do when she should fill the place as a mother. Quilts had to be made, blankets could be bought but they were not the basic covers for the beds . . . [quilts] helped one to stay warm in a house which had no weatherstripping; and really there might just be a window glass broken out, or cracks around the openings. Of course, there was only one heating stove in any of those western houses and only one bed in the room where it was. Anyway, when the late evening fire burned out, it could be mighty cold between that and the following morning when the temperature hovered around zero degrees. . . . The three girls were growing toward young womanhood and were at home in the summertime. They each got on a side [of the quilt] and quilted for some time. The mother looked over and each girl had quilted a boy's name in a corner of the quilt. She said, "As ye sew so shall ye rip; now get that mess ripped out of those corners." They had considerable teasing and hindering the work.[24]

During this time, a set of quilting frames was standard household equipment, and many older Texans readily recall growing up with a quilt always in progress. Often, frames were suspended by ropes from the ceiling and raised and lowered as necessary. It was apparently not uncommon for children to while away time in the evenings by lying on the floor and tossing things into the air to see if they would catch in the suspended quilt. Of course the next day when a long-suffering mother lowered the quilt to begin work, she would find all sorts of foreign objects littering her creation.

After 1900, the general fascination with Victorian flamboyance tapered off. The popularity of opulent crazy quilts and slumber throws declined along with it, although they appear to have remained popular in Texas for several years after the fashion died out in other parts of the country. Pieced quilts, always the most popular form of quilt in

[24] Wilna Morton Daugherty, *She Did What She Could: History of a Pioneer Woman*, pp. 90–91.

History of Quilts in Texas 33

Texas, and appliqué regained prominence among quilters of the day.

However, perhaps in the last throes of Victorian hyperbole, in 1905 the *Ladies Home Journal* published a series of designs for quilts painted by male artists. For example, one, "A Dragon Bedquilt" by Gazo Foudji, featured a Japanese-style dragon surrounded by ornate flourishes and intricate decorative borders. Maxfield Parish and Ernest Thompson Seton, among others, also contributed to the series. All of the designs are beautiful as paintings or drawings but basically unrealizable in fabric. The editors concluded the presentation of each design with the understatement "It is impossible for us to supply any patterns for this quilt. All that can be told about it is told here." No doubt the female quilt artists among the magazine's readership appreciated the comic relief.

Women's magazines, which began to have widespread distribution and enormous influence all across the United States, featured quilt patterns, articles about quiltmaking, and nostalgic illustrations of old quilts. *The Ladies' Home Journal, Woman's Home Companion, McCall's, Scribner's, Delineator,* and several other periodicals stimulated interest in quiltmaking. Farm papers such as *Farm and Fireside, National Stockman and Farmer,* and *Hearth and Home* also ran items on quilts and quilting. *The Semi-Weekly Farm News,* published in Dallas, carried quilt patterns submitted by readers. Reflecting this interest, a spate of catalogs featuring quilt patterns appeared in the decade from 1910 to 1920. One of the first, and best, books about quilts was published in 1915—Marie D. Webster's *Quilts: Their Story, and How to Make Them.*

In Texas—at the time still a predominantly agrarian state, even a pioneer society in certain areas—quiltmaking was a vital part of everyday life. The quilt had never gone out of style or use, and the surge of media attention given to quilts in the first twenty years of the century only reinforced Texas quilters' unflagging interest in their familiar, necessary activity.

When the United States entered World War I in 1917, quiltmaking received additional impetus throughout the country. The U.S. government advertised in magazines and newspapers, urging civilians to "Make Quilts—Save the Blankets for our Boys over There." The government took all the wool produced for commercial use in 1918 and instituted "heatless Mondays."[25]

In support of the war effort, the manufacture of quilts became more important than ever.

1930–41: The Depression Years

In the late 1920s and throughout the 1930s, the attention given to quilts in printed matter continued to increase. This period in quilting history is commonly regarded as a time of widespread revival of interest in quilts in North America. The severe economic hardships imposed by the Depression prompted a general return to making quilts out of necessity. The Panhandle and Plains areas of Texas formed the lower portion of the Dust Bowl, and conditions there were particularly bleak. Many people simply did not have the money to buy blankets, and women relied upon their own skills and resources to keep their families warm. Publications responded to this interest by featuring more items relating to quilts. These were eagerly awaited, read, exchanged, and saved.

In addition to magazines, newspapers—most notably the *Kansas City Star*—presented traditional and original quilt

[25] Cuesta Benberry, "The Twentieth Century's First Quilt Revival," *Quilter's Newsletter Magazine*, October, 1979, p. 10.

patterns on a regular basis. Dallas's *Semi-Weekly Farm News* carried the "Nancy Page Quilt Club" articles and offered patterns that could be ordered from the paper's home office.

Two classic books on quiltmaking appeared at this time. Ruth Finley's *Old Patchwork Quilts and the Women Who Made Them* came out in 1929, and *The Romance of the Patchwork Quilt in America* by Carrie Hall and Rose Kretsinger was published in 1936.

In the 1930s, numerous community quilting clubs were organized in Texas. Sometimes instituted as part of a county home demonstration club, these groups were formed primarily in small towns and rural areas and were an amplification of the old-time quilting bee. Although loosely structured, the clubs elected officers and set specific meeting times. Membership comprised local and area women, most of whom had been friends for years or who were related to one another in some way. They met on a regular basis to share materials and help one another make quilts for their families, thus lightening the workload for all. Quilting clubs became important as a means of social interaction and provided valuable practical and emotional support for members. In some instances, a group evolved into a profit-making enterprise, offering its quilting skills to the public for a fee. Earnings were usually donated to some community activity or charitable cause. Although time and circumstances have considerably modified the makeup of the clubs, many of them are still in operation today.

It was during the Depression that manufacturers began to actively solicit and vie for the purchasing power of quilters. Responding to the renewed interest in quilts, fabric manufacturers hired authorities to give lectures on quiltmaking to women's groups. The Taylor Bedding Company, founded in Taylor, Texas, in 1903, began to include a quilt pattern on the paper sleeve containing its Morning Glory quilt batts. One of the first two companies to market quilt batts in the United States (the other being Stearns and Foster) and still one of the nation's largest producers of batting, the Taylor Bedding Company also began to distribute in the 1930s a pamphlet containing quilt patterns and quilting techniques.

Texas celebrated the one-hundredth anniversary of her independence from Mexico in 1936. The centennial encouraged the documentation of Texas history in a variety of ways. For women, quilts were one of the prime means used to record the state's heritage. Newspapers and magazines published centennial patterns to commemorate the event, and numerous quilters created their own designs. An outline map of the state formed of patchwork counties was a popular project, and several examples of this quilt pattern can be found in Texas museums. Bluebonnets, cattle brands, and various star patterns (particularly the Lone Star) were also common.

Texas quilts dating from the 1930s frequently display a quilting design known as the "shell" or "clamshell." This design appears to have been popular throughout the South from the mid-1800s, and it was especially so in Texas. A makeshift compass was made of a piece of string tied to a pencil or some other marking device. Then the design was transferred onto a quilt top by holding the string taut at a specific point and arcing the pencil to form a half-circle. This action was repeated all over the quilt top. Because the design was marked and quilted from the quilt's edges inward, it was difficult to make the design meet in the middle. Most quilts with the shell design have a thin strip down the center marking this discontinuity. Old-time Texas quilters called this strip "the hog's back," a name that probably derives from the razorback, a type of pig once common throughout the South, which has a hairy ridge down its spine.

In a similar manner, veteran Texas quilters named their other mistakes. A knot showing on the quilt top was sometimes called a "rooster tail," while an overly large quilting stitch was dubbed a "toenail hanger."

1941–69: World War II and the Postwar Era

Throughout World War II, quiltmaking continued to be a common activity in Texas. The Red Cross war effort was frequently supported through quilting, with the "signature" quilt being especially popular for this purpose. In a signature quilt, business people, store owners, and citizens of a community would pay a small fee to have their names embroidered on quilt blocks. The blocks were then sewn together and quilted, and the finished quilt was raffled off. All proceeds were donated to the Red Cross. Red and white or red, white, and blue were the standard colors used in these Red Cross quilts, which are now fascinating community records.

Magazines carried special features on patriotic quilts. Quilters were urged to use the colors of the flag when making adaptations of old designs, rechristened with names like Three Cheers and Liberty. The February, 1941, issue of the *Farm Journal and Farmer's Wife* offered wartime patterns with the comment: "In this period, when Americans are realizing how blessed they are to be Americans, the red, white and blue combination is the most popular of all color schemes. Such a quilt, made in this period, would certainly be treasured by your descendants."[26]

After the war, however, throughout the 1950s and into the early 1960s, there was less general interest in quiltmaking in Texas than at any time since its introduction into the

[26] *Farm Journal and Farmer's Wife*, February, 1941, p. 46.

state in the early nineteenth century. The shortages of the war were over, and mass-produced goods were readily available at reasonable cost. The prevalent point of view tended away from the past and its hardships. To many, the quilt was associated with lean times and "making do." For the first time in Texas, quiltmaking had become dated and old-fashioned. This is not to say that all Texas women had stopped making quilts—but far fewer women did so.

Another factor in the decline of quiltmaking in Texas was the urbanization of the state. Following World War II, the population was no longer predominantly rural. Because quilting had always been most prevalent in rural areas, the movement from farms to cities signaled a movement away from quilts. The quilt's traditional role as a mandatory household item was virtually over.

In Texas, as in the rest of the United States and in Canada, it was primarily older quilters, those who had always quilted, who kept the art of quiltmaking alive during this period. Some younger women had begun to work outside the home during the war, and afterward many continued their careers. Because quiltmaking was no longer an economic mainstay, younger women had little time or inclination to learn. As more and more women entered the workforce, fewer and fewer learned to quilt.

1970–80: A New Era

It was the granddaughters of these older women who began to revive the current interest in quiltmaking. The back-to-the-land movement, prompted by the antimaterialism of the late 1960s, generated a desire among many young people to learn hand skills that had been neglected in the postwar rush toward an automated society. Enthusiasm for old crafts and art forms made the quilt a fashionable collector's item and sparked a renewed interest in its manufacture.

Magazines again featured numerous articles on quilts. In the early 1970s, a new dimension was added to the printed media's contributions to quiltmaking. Periodicals devoted entirely to quilts began to emerge. *Quilter's Newsletter*, established in 1969 and subtitled *The Magazine for Quilt Lovers*, dedicated itself to the promotion of quilts and quiltmaking. Other magazines followed suit. The decade saw widespread publication on every aspect of quilting. Scores of new books were written on the subject, and most of the old classics were reprinted. Quilts had become big business.

It was during the 1970s that the women's movement, in discovering and publicizing the previously ignored achievements of women throughout history, recognized the quilt's importance as an art form. In a remarkable essay entitled "Quilts: The Great American Art," first published in the *Feminist Art Journal* in 1973, Patricia Mainardi debunked the anonymity associated with quiltmakers and recognized their innovations in design and color usage. The work of Mainardi and other feminist writers exposed many people to quilts for the first time, and as women began to examine their artistic legacy, the quilt emerged as a powerful link between early and contemporary artists.

Folklorists also devoted serious study to quilts. They recognized the quilt's particular ability to reflect and define family economy, period architecture, social customs, religious beliefs, and political ideas indicative of the time and culture in which it was made.

It was the Bicentennial celebration of 1976 that galvanized the quilt revival. An appropriate symbol of the nation's cultural heritage, the quilt became extraordinarily popular as a means of expressing national pride and achievement. Many who had never before been interested in quiltmaking made a quilt as a Bicentennial project. Groups and individuals alike were attracted to the medium.

In the latter half of the 1970s in Texas as well as the rest of the country, there was a radical shift in emphasis away from quiltmaking as a household craft practiced by individuals or loosely structured community groups. In the past, quilting skills had been handed down through successive generations in the home environment. In Texas, the Second World War marked a general change in the traditional mother-daughter teaching arrangement. With a revival of interest in quilts in the early 1970s, the instruction of quiltmaking was taken over by quilt shops and community-sponsored continuing education programs. Quilt shops, which opened in most large cities, catered specifically to quilters and their needs. In addition to providing basic and advanced courses in how to make a quilt, these shops offered custom quilting services. In so doing, the quilt shops assumed the role formerly held exclusively by local quilting clubs and highly skilled individuals. Quiltmaking as a family tradition and cottage industry was replaced by quiltmaking as a full-fledged business.

Increasingly, an interest in quilts entailed participation in a highly organized activity. Quilt guilds were formed throughout Texas and the rest of the country. These guilds were formally structured groups dedicated to the continuation and advancement of the art of quiltmaking. Guild membership, while primarily urban in makeup, comprised both old and young, novices and masters, men and women, and cut across racial lines. National and regional quilting organizations were also formed.

Professional quilt authorities, similar to those of the 1930s, reappeared on an unprecedented scale. With the establishment of quilt shops and guilds in most major cities all across the United States and Canada, and through publicity provided by quilt-related publications, a market was created for a North American lecture and workshop circuit directed at quilters. Authors of successful books on quilting—along with quilt artists, quilt designers, and quilt historians—found a large, receptive national audience. In symposiums, festivals, and training sessions sponsored by shops and guilds, these professionals traveled from coast to coast demonstrating their individual expertise. One of the largest of these festivals is held annually in Houston and attracts nationally known instructors and professional exhibitors, as well as visitors from all over the country.

Although the future of quiltmaking in Texas appears to be linked to shops, guilds, and the growing national quilt network, the state's traditional church and community quilting groups still exist. In all likelihood however, these groups will not regenerate themselves when current members die or retire. With their roots firmly entrenched in rural Texas and their membership composed primarily of older, lifetime homecraft quilters, they are not likely to attract many recruits from younger urban fabric artists.

Whatever direction quiltmaking takes in Texas, it is certain that the art has a solid future in the state. Interest in quilts and their creation is high; literally hundreds of Texans of all ages are learning to quilt. One Houston quilt shop alone has taught the art to more than two thousand people during a four-year period. More and more guilds are being established, and membership is growing rapidly, while long-established quilting clubs still operate.

Today the quilt not only binds us to our past but also provides continuous, tangible evidence of women's culture in Texas. Jane Long and the hundreds of pioneer women of all backgrounds who followed her would not feel particularly out of place with modern-day quilters. Many of the traditional patterns of the 1980s were in use in the early 1800s, and many of the quilting techniques currently in vogue are basically the same as those popular in frontier days. Economic necessity no longer dictates the quilt's contruction, but an equally powerful impetus—as strong today as it was in early Texas—is still at work: the creative urge.

Throughout its relatively brief history in Texas, the quilt has been an important part of life in the state; its makers, "eternally the conservators of civilization," have contributed inestimably to a rich and varied heritage. The quilt will remain a powerful reminder of our past and a fitting symbol of the future of Texas women and their work.

CHAPTER 2

Lone Star Quilters

"Honey, if I didn't quilt I'd go crazy. My hands has got to be busy. The only time my hands is idle is when I'm asleep. And you'd be surprised at what I think about when I sit there and quilt. I go way back in my mind and dig out things. Sometimes I laugh and sometimes I cry. You see a little piece of material that reminds you of things—they just come to your memory. I remember when I was a certain age. One of my sisters and I—we were tomboys. We used to climb trees, ride steers, just about anything a boy would do, but we dare not let our mother know. We had a big barn with log beams going across it and we'd climb up on those logs and walk across the width of the barn. One day when we did that I had on a brand-new dress. It was made of real tough material because that's the kind we had to wear. And I got up on that log and walked across the barn, but I fell off. Well, the hem of my dress caught on a nail and I hung there in the air. My sister just sat there and laughed. A scrap of that dress was in one of the quilts that I pieced. I saw it the other day and I thought about all those things."[1]

—Mabel Payne
Austin, Texas

"When I was eight or nine years old, my grandmother taught me how to quilt. She lived right down here behind me—the old house is still standing there. The first time I quilted, it was in the spring of the year. It come up a cloud—a shower

[1] Mabel Payne, interview with author, Austin, February 8, 1979.

cloud—and you know how they'll do. It was thunderin' and blowin' and eventually it come a streak of lightnin' and it hit the flue to Grandma's cookstove. It throwed brick all over that house. Boy, oh boy, it even throwed brick on the quilt. It's a wonder it didn't electrocute us. She had put that quilt in just special for me to learn how to quilt. She'd say, 'No, Hon, you made too big a stitch here. Now take it out and make a little stitch.' Guess she wondered when that lightnin' hit whether she was doin' the right thing."[2]

—Bea Strawn
Lytton Springs, Texas

"We lived on a ranch in San Saba County. I grew up with a quilt hangin' from the ceilin', ready to be worked on when time could be spared from the other chores. It was a way of life for us to have a quilt in the makin'. Mama would engage in quiltin' in the afternoons, before supper. And it didn't matter if a quilt was kept hangin' there all year long—we'd take one down and put up another one. We quilted all year 'round, and a lot of times, for pure sociability, we'd have a quilting bee. There were lots of bees then—corn husking bees, or onion peeling bees and the like—and the neighbors would all come over to help. Mama would have a great big ol' cake cooked and we'd make a gallon of homemade ice cream and when the work was through we'd all sit down and have ice cream and cake and talk and visit. Somebody would have a fiddle or a guitar and maybe there would be dancin' and music. Quiltin' was a thing you grew up with. You just learned how to do it, just like cookin', and washin' and anything else, and you knew someday you'd do your own."[3]

—Loree Templeton
Austin, Texas

[2]Bea Strawn, interview with author, Lytton Springs, February 19, 1979.
[3]Loree Templeton, interview with author, Austin, March 9, 1979.

"I was born just a little below here at Manchaca, but I grew up here and I got my schoolin' here. My mother and daddy had a four-hundred–acre ranch and farm about two miles over this way and then my husband moved here in 1911. I came home with his sister one evenin' from school and she introduced me to her older brother. He was out at the wood-pile choppin' wood, and I said to myself, 'Now, that one's mine even if I never get him.' But I got him, and then I didn't know what to do with him! Oh, he had the prettiest red hair that just laid in waves on his head. He was older than I was—he was about twenty-five and I guess I would've been sixteen. He had a brand-new rubber-tire buggy with a fine, big bay horse. I ended up marryin' him, of course. He smoked Duke's tobacco and it came in little cloth sacks. Back then, now I'm tellin' you, it was hard times and things was scarce. I didn't want to throw all them little sacks away because they was good material—unbleached domestic. So I saved enough of 'em to make a quilt. I had to rip the seams out and wash 'em and iron 'em. And after I dyed 'em I had to iron 'em again. I dyed 'em three colors—pink and green and yellow. There's a bush, algerita, some folks call it, and the roots makes the most beautiful yellow dye you ever seen. It made a pretty quilt. My husband kept sayin', 'Why I wouldn't fool with them things if I was you. That's too much trouble.' But after he seen what I done with 'em, he was kinda pleased about it."[4]

—Fannie McIntyre
Driftwood, Texas

"My mother was always quilting. She'd piece [quilts] out of scraps from our clothes. She'd see a pattern in a paper or a magazine and she'd cut it out and get to work on it. She'd

---

[4] Fannie McIntyre, interview with author, Driftwood, March 19, 1979.

use a page of a Sears-Roebuck catalogue to make the pattern. We always thought that all the quilts she made were pretty. And us kids would stand around and watch while she was quilting. I'd see a piece of fabric in the quilt and I'd say, 'Oh, this was my dress.' And my brother would say, 'Well, that's my shirt.' And my younger sister would come along and say, 'This is my dress here, and that's my bonnet over there.' We always looked to see who had what in the quilt. It tied you together somehow."[5]

—Frieda Dailey
Austin, Texas

Perhaps never again in Texas will the quilt have so immediate and basic a significance as it does to these women and others like them. They will be the last to have considered the quilt a necessity, the last to regard it in so social a context, the last to know it on such familiar, everyday terms.

They are part of a Texas tradition that included women from many different races and cultures and all walks of life. As long as women have constituted a considerable portion of the population in Texas, quilts have been a manifest part of the lifestyle. Virtually everyone used them in the early days of the state's history, and quiltmaking was an activity common to humble and high-ranking households alike.

Texas folklore reflects the prevalence of quiltmaking in the state. In Texas, as in other parts of the South, a custom called "cat shaking" was associated with quilts. This ritual was enacted when unmarried girls were among the quilters on hand when a finished quilt was taken out of the frames. The girls were told to hold the corners of the quilt while a cat was placed in the middle. When the quilt was shaken, the cat naturally jumped out. According to superstition, the

[5] Frieda Dailey, interview with author, Austin, February 16, 1979.

girl standing nearest the point where the cat jumped out of the quilt would be the next to marry. Some say that the cat needed to be black in order for the magic to work. This custom was apparently most common in North Texas, although it was followed throughout the state. Another superstition held that a woman who pricked her fingers while quilting would get a kiss for each prick.

Evidence of the broad appeal of quiltmaking in Texas can be found in museums all across the state and in historical records. The Sam Houston Historical Museum in Huntsville contains a set of quilting frames that belonged to Margaret Lea Houston, Sam Houston's wife.

Texas' first woman of letters was a quilter. Mary Austin Holley, cousin of Stephen F. Austin, paid a visit to her famous relative's colony in 1831. While there she wrote what her publisher described as "the first book published in English on Texas." *Texas: Observations, Historical, Geographical and Descriptive in a Series of Letters* came out in 1833. That the author made quilt tops is documented in a letter in which she describes a bout with cholera. "I was myself seized with spasms after I had gone to bed. I felt the circulation arrested and coldness fast spreading over me like the chill of death. . . . At this instant I heard the Doctor, who never left us. . . . He ran up and gave me ether, peppermint, & hot brandy toddy & with my feet in the fire, and a hot flat-iron which happened to be there (thanks to my patchwork) at my breast, & friction of the hands, after keeping the Doctor and Madam Hermogene with me the greatest part of the night, I went quietly to bed again."[6]

Aunt Sophia Porter, who entertained Robert E. Lee and Ulysses S. Grant in the fledgling days of Texas statehood,

[6]W. C. Nunn, "Mary Austin Holley," in *Women of Texas*, p. 45.

XIT Ranch Autograph Quilt, ca. 1938–41; pieced and handpainted; satin; 96"x84". By Mrs. J. Luther Ramsey, Hereford. From the collection of the Panhandle-Plains Historical Museum, Canyon, by permission.

One of the most famous of Texas' ranches is commemorated in this quilt, which features autographs and comments of XIT cowboys.

Crazy Quilt, 1888; pieced and appliqué with embroidery; silk, satin, velvet, taffeta, and brocade; 86″x71″. By Pauline Rilling, San Antonio. From the collection of the San Antonio Museum Association, by permission.

Crazy quilts, so named for an ob-vious reason, were popular in Texas and throughout the nation from the 1880s to the turn of the century. This lavish example won first prize in the textiles division of the 1888 San Antonio International Exposition.

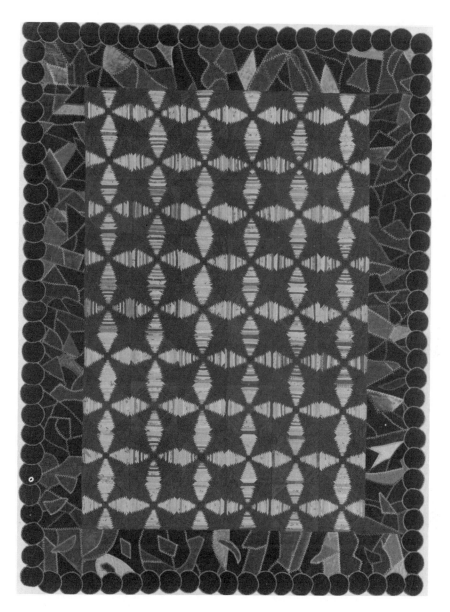

Pineapple, ca. 1885–90; pieced slumber-throw; velvet, satin, silk, and taffeta; 71½"x52½". By Jane Lyons Roberts, San Antonio. From the collection of the San Antonio Museum Association, by permission.

While the fabrics chosen and the irregular shapes and decorative stitching of the border reflect some of the same influences as the Crazy Quilt, the central pattern is a traditional, if somewhat uncommon, one.

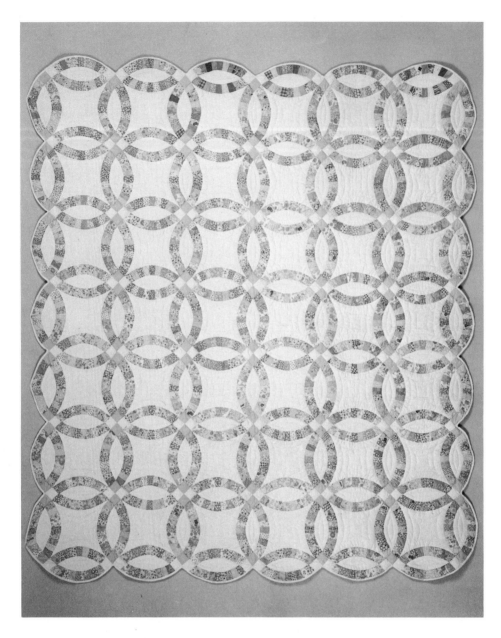

Double Wedding Ring, ca. 1930–40; pieced; cotton; 84"x72". By Miriam A. Ferguson, Austin. From the collection of George Nalle, Jr. Photograph by Jack Puryear.

This quilt, done in a traditional pattern by Texas' only woman governor, helps indicate the nearly universal popularity of quilts among Texas women until only a few decades ago. In her creation, Mrs. Ferguson used pink solid patches and multicolored calicos on an unbleached muslin background.

Texas Bluebonnet, 1936; pieced and appliqué; cotton; 83"x72". Raffle quilt made by the Home Demonstration Club, Lockhart. Won and owned by Mrs. Jack Thurman, Austin. Photograph by Jack Puryear.

A number of themes associated with the State of Texas have been prominent in Texas quiltmaking in the twentieth century. Texas Bluebonnet was a Texas Centennial quilt pattern marketed in a kit. Mrs. Thurman remembers that tickets on this quilt sold for twenty-five cents apiece or five for a dollar. She liked the quilt when she saw it and bought a ticket for a quarter, even though "things were tight."

Bicentennial Quilt, 1976; appliqué; cotton; 107″x73″. By the San Antonio Needlework Guild. From the collection of the San Antonio Museum Association, by permission.

The twenty-four blocks of this quilt depict San Antonio landmarks, ranching, oil development, and military interests, as well as native wild flowers and birds. The American Bicentennial emblem is in the center of the quilt.

wrote that a quilt figured prominently in the decor of her first home. "We lived in a clapboard house with puncheon floors, and our table consisted of a goods box with legs on it. I picked with my own fingers the cotton for the first quilt I had in Grayson County; and when it was ready, Colonel Coffee laid the quilt off with a square and I quilted it. I then made me a rag carpet and put it on the puncheon floor, and a goods box nailed up on the side of the wall was my wardrobe. And on viewing my carpet, quilt, and wardrobe, I was the happiest woman in Texas."[7]

This same Aunt Sophia was known as "the Paul Revere of Grayson County" in North Texas. During the Civil War a group of Northern soldiers stopped at her home and demanded rooms for the night. She agreed and opened her wine cellar to them as well. While the men were drinking, she slipped out of the house, saddled a mule, and rode twenty-five miles to warn Confederate troops of the Yankees' arrival. According to the story, her mission required that she ford a river. Soaking wet, she stopped on the other side at a neighbor's home. There she borrowed a quilt to wrap up in for the remainder of her journey.[8]

A beautiful girl known as Frenchy McCormick, "the shrewdest monte dealer in the West," wore a patchwork skirt. Frenchy lived in the wild Panhandle boom town of Tascosa, in the district known as Hog Town. During the 1880s, Tascosa was noted for its dance halls, saloons, rowdy characters (such as Billy the Kid), and a cemetery called Boothill. In these surroundings, Frenchy would sit at the gaming tables, attired in her patchwork skirt, a spangled blouse, and red shoes. It is said that she rarely spoke to any-

[7] Winnie Allen and Carrie Walker Allen, *Pioneering in Texas: True Stories of the Early Days*, p. 80.
[8] Ibid., p. 89.

one except her talking parrot, which hung in a cage at the back of the saloon.[9]

An original-design quilt made by the great-grandmother of President Lyndon Johnson can be seen at the Lyndon B. Johnson National Historic Site in Stonewall. At the Dwight D. Eisenhower Birthplace Museum in Denison is a Tumbling Blocks quilt made by the former president's mother, supposedly with the help of her sons.

In the 1930s, Miriam A. ("Ma") Ferguson, Texas' first and only woman governor, tried her hand at quiltmaking, using the traditional double-wedding-ring pattern. Governor Ferguson was a skilled needlewoman, and her quilt, which now belongs to her grandson, George Nalle, Jr., of Austin, is an esteemed family heirloom.

Mrs. Charles Bybee of Houston and the late Ima Hogg, both noted philanthropists, recognized the value and importance of the needle arts to Texas history, and both women assembled fine collections of quilts. Miss Hogg donated part of her holdings to the University of Texas for the Winedale Historical Center, while many of Mrs. Bybee's quilts are on public display at Henkel Square in Round Top. Hundreds of less well-known individuals have donated family quilts to museums throughout the state. This grassroots acknowledgment of the importance of quilts and their makers attests to the contribution of both to life and culture in Texas.

The quilt has entered the twentieth-century consciousness like a familiar melody. It hangs in galleries, serves as subject matter for poems and plays and books, and decorates our homes in every conceivable form. Just as every melody has a composer, so every quilt has a maker. And just as the identities of the composers of many of our most popu-

[9]Willie Newbury Lewis, *Between Sun and Sod: An Informal History of the Texas Panhandle*, p. 44.

lar traditional songs have been obscured by the dim, anonymity of "public domain," so the quiltmaker has too often
suffered a similar fate. Yet we can see her work, touch it, and
be touched by it in return. And although in many cases she
will remain faceless and unknown, it is still the maker who
imbues the random bits of fabric with the particular quality
that belongs to her quilt alone.

"I remember when I's makin' quilts for my grandchil-
dren. I had to buy material because I had run out of scraps
by that time. My husband told me that I was gonna wear
out my shoes a walkin' downtown tryin' to match material
to get the right color. I walked down 6th Street huntin'
prints. I fixed 'em shaded, you know, kind of in a rainbow
style. I'd start with the light color and work out to the dark.
I'd put one solid row and then the next row would be a figured that went with it. I'd walk and walk the streets of Austin tryin' to find a certain color. I didn't like any of the big
figures. I liked the small little prints. It was worth it though.
I figure it'll give 'em all somethin' to remember me by."[10]

—Myrtle Ward
Austin, Texas

[10] Myrtle Ward, interview with author, Austin, February 1, 1979.

CHAPTER 3

Group Quilting and Cultural Influence

Quiltmaking is a variable art form. Within a given structure, it is always changing, always adapting, always being altered slightly to meet the creative criteria of the individual maker. The example is often cited of the numerous names given a single quilt pattern—a practice reflecting the diverse geographic, political, and cultural backgrounds of quilters. Thus the pattern known as the Star of Bethlehem in New England became the Lone Star in Texas, and the Colonial Rose was rechristened the Yellow Rose of Texas. No two quilts are ever exactly alike; each is a manifestation of its creator's unique sensibilities. At the same time, every quilt is a composite of the collective traditions of quiltmaking that have gone before.

The process of quiltmaking allows for great freedom of personal expression, not only in the nature of the quilt itself but also in the way it is made. The same medium that provides a vehicle for "social" art also nurtures the "lone" quilter, whose joy and proficiency in making something beautiful demand that she not risk spoiling her creation by sharing the work with someone less skilled. It is an indication of the fluid nature of the process that a quilt is frequently a harmonious blend of individual and collective efforts.

A quilt top, usually pieced by one person, is often quilted by a group of women working together. This group aspect is one of the characteristics that distinguishes quiltmaking from other needle arts. The social appeal as well as the practicality of joining with others to finish a task have made group quilting one of the most enduring of North America's cultural traditions.

By nature, the steps involved in making a quilt in the traditional manner (that is, completing an entire top and then quilting it in a frame) divide along individual and group lines. The first step, that of making the top, is more effectively accomplished by one person. Both the manageability of the work and the decision making required are well suited to individual effort. A quilt top is most commonly made up of units, or blocks, sewn together to form a pattern. Sizes of blocks vary from pattern to pattern, but none is so large as to preclude its being "lap" work for one person.

The aesthetic choices required in making a top—pattern, color combination, fabric, quilting design, and size— lend themselves to an individual's creative preferences. Once all of these fundamental decisions have been made and the blocks have been sewn together to complete the top, it is easier and faster to have help with the second step, the actual quilting.

The work involved in quilting is not easily manageable for one person. Putting the finished top into frames to be quilted is a big job—one more efficiently handled by many hands. In addition, quilting itself is a time-consuming process; the more people doing the task, the more quickly it goes. Because all of the major creative choices have been made by the time a top is ready to be quilted, the plans of the individual maker can be easily carried out by a group.

Instances of an entire quilt—both piecing and quilting—being a group project are not rare, but certainly they are specific in nature. There are three standard types of group quilt: (1) a friendship quilt, in which a number of people contribute individual signed blocks of the same design to form a top; (2) a friendship album or medley, a quilt made when a number of people contribute blocks of different patterns, often united by a color theme; or (3) "event" quilts, which are made by a group for some particular occasion, such as the Bicentennial, a community celebration, or a fund-raising activity. But traditionally, by far the most common case is that of one person making a top and a group of people quilting it.

Group interaction is so basic to the art of quiltmaking that it has influenced the establishment of specific types of quilting groups. In direct relation to the growth and structuring of Texas society, quilting groups have evolved from one another. Undoubtedly, the first type of quilting group comprised family members, and as the population increased, neighbors augmented the family group during "bees." The founding of towns gave rise to church and community quilting organizations. The permanence of institution and place added structure and purpose to these groups, in that regular meeting times and goals (usually fund raising) were often set. In more recent times, urbanization and government programs have prompted the formation of quilt guilds and senior citizens' clubs, which have even more formal structure.

The interesting thing about these various groupings is that although they developed from one another, they never canceled each other out. Each type actively exists in its original form. It is still common practice in Texas for mothers, daughters, and other relatives to quilt together, and it is not unusual for a family quilting group to include male relatives on occasion. Quilting bees continue in much the same way as they traditionally have. Their social significance has diminished, of course, as rural isolation has lessened, but there are still informal and irregular gatherings of friends and neighbors to help a particular woman quilt a top. As always, that woman prepares a meal or refreshments for the quilters.

Community quilting groups are popular in small towns all across the state. The groups are less rural than those that hold quilting bees and are slightly more structured. They function like clubs, with officers, a treasury, and usually a central meeting place, such as a Masonic Hall or a school cafeteria. A particular day is set aside for quilting by the group, and each member brings something to eat, rather than having an entire meal prepared by one person. Many of these groups, such as the Lytton Springs Quilting Club, have been meeting together for years and have become important contributors to their communities.

Church quilting groups remain active throughout Texas. Membership is always drawn from the church, but the amount and type of structure vary from group to group. Some of these quilting groups are formal offshoots of church auxiliary organizations, while others have no structure whatsoever and meet only when the need arises. In addition to fund-raising work, that is, quilting finished tops for a fee, some church groups make entire quilts for specific purposes. For example, the high school seniors in a congregation might be given friendship quilts to commemorate their graduation, as is the case at the Lawrence Avenue Church of Christ in Anton. Church quilting groups have been common in Texas since the last quarter of the 1800s, and at least one has been in continuous operation since before the turn of the century. The Grace United Methodist Church Quilting Club in Austin has been meeting regularly since 1897.

In recent years, federally financed senior citizens' programs have mobilized the time and skills of older quilters throughout the state. The resulting senior citizens' quilting clubs serve as a lesson in the power of collective endeavor. In Austin a group of this type regularly makes quilts for needy families, while a club in Dripping Springs has earned enough money to help build a senior citizens' activity center. In Blanco, after federal funding for a senior citizens' group ran out, one of its members bought a local building and hired on her quilting friends at the rate of seventy-five cents an hour. Their quilts are sold to the public, and the profits are used to defray expenses.

During the last decade, an urban counterpart for the rural community quilting group has been established. Quilt guilds now operate in most of the larger cities in Texas. Members include a cross section of novices and experts, traditional and contemporary stylists, collectors, artists, craftspeople, and all-around quilt devotees. In addition to the shared interest, creative exchange, and social activity common to all quilting groups, the guilds provide a link to the larger arena of quiltmaking—the national speaker-workshop circuit.

A common thread binding all these types of groups is that of friendship. Particularly in the case of older women, a quilting group provides emotional support, a sense of purpose, and significant social interaction. In the atmosphere of group activity, individual ills and loneliness are forgotten. These groupings are by no means rigid or exclusive. Most quilters simply like to quilt and will do so at every opportunity in a variety of groups and settings.

In Texas, quilting groups—particularly church clubs— are, however, occasionally delineated along racial or cultural lines. Every member of the Holy Ghost Lutheran Church Sewing Circle in Fredericksburg (in operation since 1922) speaks German as a native language, while the joint quilting club of the Saint Emanuel Baptist Church and other Baptist churches in Hearne is made up entirely of black quilters. It is in such settings that ethnic influences are most apt to be evident in the design or pattern of a quilt.

Texas is fortunate in having a population made up of remarkably diverse cultures. A history of government under the flags of six nations and liberal immigration laws throughout the nineteenth century guaranteed the state a varied, "melting-pot" society. A number of these ethnic groups have developed and maintained a particular affinity for quiltmaking, and their influence on the individual creative act is another aspect of the social nature of quilting. The ethnic heritage of a particular group naturally affects and governs the attitudes and behavior of individuals within that group. Thus, when a Mexican-American woman makes a quilt, her aesthetic choices may reflect a heritage of the *colchas bordadas* (embroidered blankets) of Mexico. Similarly, a woman from the Rio Grande Valley recalled how her grandmother, who was an Indian, quilted on an upright frame—always out-of-doors—in much the same way as Navajo women weave blankets.[1]

A link between *colchas bordadas* and other embroidered textiles belonging to the Mexican culture can be seen in the appliquéd quilts of Virginia Quintanilla of San Antonio.[2] The octogenarian grandmother has been making quilts since 1935. Married at fourteen, she spent her honeymoon picking cotton, and since then she has been employed constantly in an amazing variety of occupations. For the past twenty years she has earned a living by making quilts, quilting tops, and making *cascarones*, colorful, confetti-filled eggshells used for Easter celebrations, weddings, and festivals. Mrs. Quintanilla makes pieced as well as appliquéd quilts, and in both types, even though she uses traditional Anglo-American designs, her heritage is evident. Her personal preference for the juxtaposition of vibrant colors is a cultural

---

[1]Minerva De Leon, interview with author, Austin, February 13, 1980.
[2]Virginia Quintanilla, interview with author, San Antonio, October 18, 1980.

preference as well, one that can be seen in Mexican-American arts and crafts ranging from paper flowers to mosaic murals. When Mrs. Quintanilla's use of brilliant colors is coupled with an overlay of embroidery, the effect is striking. The use of embroidery with appliqué is certainly not unique to Mrs. Quintanilla, but her choice of that particular technique does seem rooted in an ethnic tradition.

Black women have an especially rich heritage of quilt-making. Their ancestors, who were brought to the United States as slaves, were skilled in African needle arts. Those women who could weave and sew brought high prices at slave auctions, and many slave women were taught the art of quilting and given the job of making quilts for a plantation. The dominant culture dictated the types of quilt patterns that were chosen for general use, but in making quilts for their own families, the slave women often gave their African background free rein. Vibrant color combinations and powerful designs displayed their legacy. Roland Freeman's photographs have captured these characteristics in the work of contemporary black quilters in Mississippi.[3]

When pioneers moved west, those who came from the southern United States brought their slaves with them. A majority of immigrants to Texas were from the South, and when Texas joined the Union, it did so as a slave state. The slave women who came to Texas already knew how to make quilts, and they handed the knowledge down through generations of daughters.

Some of the most innovative and resourceful uses of materials to be found in any medium can be seen in quilts made by blacks. Nothing useful was thrown away. Their "shirttail," "dresstail," and "necktie" quilts are self-explanatory. "Stomach" quilts were made from that part of a woman's

[3]Rosemary L. Bray and Roland F. Freeman, "Keepsakes," *Essence*, November, 1978, pp. 106–14.

dress usually covered by an apron, and hence less likely to wear out. Dresstails, shirttails, and "stomachs" were of course often used together in one quilt. Ingenious baby quilts were crafted using the tops of men's heavy work socks. When the sock feet were worn out, the good tops were cut off, split, and sewn together to form a quilt top. Batting and lining were added, and the baby had a soft, washable cover. "Britches" quilts seem to have been one of the most common types of quilt made for everyday use by black quilters in Texas. As the name implies, these quilts were made from parts of pants that had not worn out, and they were not only warm but extremely durable as well. When Matilda Brown of Manor was asked whether she had ever made a britches quilt, she was incredulous. "Lord, child!" she said. "That's the wrong question to be askin' me. You should say, how *many* britches quilts have I made. And then I'd say, I don't know. I'm eighty-two years old an' I done lost count!"[4]

When using traditional Anglo-American patterns, black quilters often interject color combinations that reflect their distinct heritage. Susan Roach Langford has noted the traits of high-contrast colors and unpredictability in the quilts made by black women in Louisiana and elsewhere.[5] Dutch Doll and Dutch Boy patterns, along with the Nine-Patch, Flower Garden, and Lone Star seem to be favorite traditional Anglo-American patterns among black quilters in Texas. It is the String quilt, however, that is probably the most culturally significant expression.

Scholars have linked the black American String quilt (which has wide distribution throughout black communities

[4]Ada Simonds, Austin, telephone conversation with author, August 1, 1980; Carrie Ross, Hearne, telephone conversation with author, September 8, 1980; Matilda Brown, Manor, telephone conversation with author, October 7, 1980.

[5]Susan Roach Langford, *Patchwork Quilts: Deep South Traditions*, p. 7.

in the United States) to the woven textiles of West Africa. The strip pattern is a traditional design element in West African art. There men weave long, narrow strips of cloth that are sewn together to make a larger piece of fabric, and women in West and Central Africa incorporate a strip pattern into their woven cloth. According to John Vlach, "The correlation between patterns in African textiles and Afro-American quilts may . . . reflect a transatlantic continuity of aesthetic preferences."[6]

Throughout the United States today, quiltmaking seems to be practiced only by the older black women. One young woman, lamenting the fact that she had never learned the art, explained, "Quilting seemed to me a plantation holdover, an antebellum embarrassment like singing 'Negro' spirituals or eating watermelon. Up against the wall, Aunt Jemima, I shouted with upraised fist. I'd rather buy a blanket. . . . I didn't understand then that all of our culture is valuable, that it should be honored not only for what it's done for us, but what it can continue to do—enrich and encourage us."[7]

Quilts are a traditional part of Afro-American culture. In addition to general household use, quilts were valuable as items of trade or barter. Black midwives often received quilts in payment for their services. There are numerous references in black literature to quilts or quilting.[8] One superstition associated with quilts comes from black midwives in North Texas. According to the lore, a newborn, unbathed

[6]John Michael Vlach, "Quilting," in *The Afro-American Tradition in Decorative Arts*, pp. 43–76.

[7]Bray and Freeman, "Keepsakes," pp. 106, 112.

[8]Lorece P. Williams, "Country Black," in *The Folklore of Texan Cultures*, ed. Francis C. Abernethy, p. 126. See also J. Mason Brewer, "Tales from Juneteenth—Elijah's Leaving Time," in *Folklore of Texan Cultures*, ed. Abernethy, pp. 116–17; Julia Peterkin, "The Quilting," in *Black April*, pp. 159–79; Toni Morrison, *Song of Solomon*, p. 6; Alice Walker, "Everyday Use," in *Black-Eyed Susans*, ed. Mary Helen Washington, pp. 86–87.

baby should be wrapped in an old quilt and marched through all the rooms of the house. This is supposed to keep the child from having measles, wetting the bed, and generally making life hard on its mother.[9]

Among Texans of Germanic and Slavic ancestry, quiltmaking has been popular for generations. According to their descendants, quiltmaking was an art form acquired by German, Norwegian, and Czech immigrants after their arrival in Texas. Mrs. Wesley Franz of Fredericksburg, a third-generation German-Texan, states that although the German word *decke* is used to describe a quilt, she knows of no German word for quilting. She maintains that among Texans of German descent, the word *quilting* is used regardless of whether a conversation is in English or German.[10]

Mrs. Milton Brown of Clifton, whose heritage is Norwegian, says: "I correspond with several relatives in Norway. They don't even know what a quilt is. Once a Norwegian Consul . . . was visiting here with friends, and I asked him what I should tell my relatives when they ask, 'What is a quilt?' After some thought, he replied: '*Lap Teppe*.' *Lap* is a scrap or patch, *teppe* is a coverlet. We spent a week in Norway and another week in Sweden and Denmark. We never saw a quilt." Mrs. Vincent Kopecky of Galveston writes that "there is no quilting in Czechoslovakia. People sleep under featherbeds there all the year around, as the nights are cool there even in summer. Our Czech women never saw a quilt until they migrated here. They soon learned quilting from the Southern ladies, since it was too hot to sleep under their featherbeds in summer. They raised their own cotton and neighbors got together to do quilting. I pieced my first quilt

[9]Tressa Turner, "The Human Comedy in Folk Superstitions," in *Straight Texas*, ed. J. Frank Dobie and Mody C. Boatright, p. 147.
[10]Mrs. Wesley Franz, interview with author, Fredericksburg, October 28, 1980.

by hand when I was ten years old, and I've sewed quilts all my life. Am 81 now."[11]

There seem to have been no particular cultural adaptations or interpretations made by these latter groups with regard to quilts. Patterns, coloration, and form all adhere to Anglo-American traditions. But the art has been adopted wholeheartedly, and quilts have definitely become a part of the culture of Germanic and Slavic Texans.

The variety of groups that participate in quiltmaking illustrates the art form's powerful ability to communicate. Quilts make statements about their makers' purposes, talents, sensibilities, and backgrounds—whether the significant identity is individual, collective, cultural, ethnic, or some combination of these. History, religion, and politics are clearly revealed through quilts, as are fashion trends, social climate, economic status, and popular culture. Quiltmaking brings people together and encourages them to talk, work with one another, exchange ideas, and share memories. Those who make quilts always do so with the intention that others will use and appreciate their creations. Maker and user are thus connected in a number of emotional and functional ways, touching one another across generations and across cultures.

One longtime Texas quilter describes her quilts as "magic carpets." They take her back to the past when the pieced scraps were dresses or shirts still in use, or forward to the future when she is piecing a baby quilt for an anticipated birth. Quilting with friends keeps her aware of the present, and, at the same time, links her to a unique cultural tradition that transcends time.

[11]Mrs. Milton Brown, letter to author, Clifton, April 7, 1980; Mrs. Vincent Kopecky, letter to author, Galveston, March 3, 1980. However the Museum of the Supreme Lodge of the Slavonic Benevolent Order of the State of Texas in Temple has a quilt that was said to have been made by Czechs in Europe in the late nineteenth century.

CHAPTER 4

Picking Up the Threads: The Contemporary Scene

Alta Vincent was a quiltmaker from the Texas Panhandle who made satin quilts for movie stars like Lillian Gish in the 1930s. Alta's special-order quilts were commissioned through a relative who owned a store in Hollywood, and, according to that relative, buyers were always amazed that someone was interested enough in quilts to spend time making them.

Many Texans have a similar reaction when they learn of the current groundswell of interest in quilts. Enough quilts have been littered with picnic leftovers, wrapped around ice cream freezers, and used as horse blankets or dog beds to dull almost anyone's esteem. That such a fuss should be made over something so familiar comes as quite a surprise to many.

In fact, however, the quilt is more popular and certainly more appreciated now than at any time in its history. This newfound respect arises from a wide variety of sources, ranging from an increased awareness of women's traditional art forms to current fashions in interior decoration. Accompanying the quilt's broadened appeal is a new kind of group involvement: the quilt guild. The growing trend toward participation in a formally organized quilt guild is the most important influence on present-day quiltmaking in Texas. Throughout the state and all across North America, guilds are providing the focus and continuity necessary to ensure that the quilt revival of the 1970s will be more than a passing wave of nostalgia. Through education, special activities, and the stimulation provided by a grass-roots communications network, guilds are fostering a large group of people who are particularly knowledgeable about quilts. This trend is a new approach to quiltmaking in Texas, and it marks a distinct departure from the ordinarily isolated, rural-based quilting clubs still common in the state.

Quiltmaking has always lent itself to group participation. A quilt guild, however, changes the nature of the group interaction while adding several new dimensions to it. In a guild, actual quilting is no longer the primary activity of the group as it is in a traditional quilting club. In fact, quilting plays a secondary role to the study and appreciation of all aspects of quilts and their creation.

This shift in interest is characteristic of all Texas guilds. Clearly it influenced Anita Murphy, founder of the Golden Triangle Quilt Guild, which represents a three-county area in southeast Texas. In publicizing her desire to start a guild she explained: "It just wouldn't be quilting like a quilting bee. I would like to have guest speakers come in and demonstrate new techniques. . . . It would be an educational get-together and we could also exchange ideas. It wouldn't be just limited to women either. There are many men who are good at quilting and I would love to have them as part of the group."[1]

The difference in purpose between guilds and clubs is usually implied by the names of such groups, as in *quilt* or *quilter's* guild versus *quilting* club, which underscores the respective emphases on broad study by the former and a particular activity by the latter. Many of the substantive differences between the two types of groups can be seen as contrasting perspectives: urban versus rural, art versus craft, and modern versus traditional.

[1] *Beaumont Enterprise-Journal*, November 23, 1980, p. 148.

Texas under Six Flags, 1936; yo-yo; silk; 84″x72″. Designed and made by Leila Chaney, Hallettsville. From the collection of Ray and Sheri Chaney. Photograph by Jack Puryear.

This quilt is made entirely of yo-yo's, small circles of fabric gathered around the edges to form puffed rounds. Its patriotic Centennial theme is, in fact, carried out with more than ten thousand yo-yo's of varying sizes. The artist's son recalls his mother working on the quilt by lamplight during the Depression. In addition to the flags and historic sites—the Capitol, the Alamo, a Spanish monk, and a covered wagon—there are representations of the contemporary scene—F.D.R., a car, and a barnstormer airplane.

Longhorns on the Chisholm Trail, 1979; pieced and appliqué; cotton; 90"x72". Designed and made by Helen Blackstone, Austin. From the collection of the artist. Photograph by Greg White, courtesy of *Texas Highways* magazine.

A traditional Texas symbol, the longhorn, provides the motif for this work of art. Each element of the quilt has significance. According to the art-ist, the printed greenish fabric "represents the lush green grass" on which the cattle were fattened before being driven up the Chisholm Trail. The rust-colored flowered print represents the rocky areas of the trip and the wild flowers passed along the way. The beige fabric suggests the clouds of dust the passing herds kicked up.

Quilt guilds and quilting clubs have a parallel—and seldom overlapping—existence. The two groups approach quiltmaking from quite different angles and attract dissimilar followings. Each in its own way fosters the art of making quilts, but they are completely unlike in concept, purpose, and structure. Perhaps the most significant point that can be made in distinguishing clubs from guilds is that the former has its roots in the past while the latter is contemporary in every respect. Consequently, a comparison of the two types of groups reveals a great deal about both the history and the future of quiltmaking in Texas.

The quilting club in Texas is very much a product of rural life in the state. Popular for over one hundred years, such groups have changed hardly at all during that time. Casual in structure and homogeneous in composition, the traditional quilting club is primarily a social organization built around shared activity and occurring in a limited situation, such as a small community, a particular church congregation, or, more recently, a senior citizens' group. For the most part, quilting clubs are small (five to fifteen members) and self-contained units that rarely make contact with other such groups. Guests are always welcome, the atmosphere is invariably friendly, and anyone may join, but no special effort is made to solicit members.

The club's single occupation is quilting, whether it be for a member (to share work) or for a nonmember (to earn money for some charitable cause). The essential by-product of this activity is social interaction. Members tend to be older women, a large percentage of whom are widows. The companionship of friends and peers, along with the activity offered by the quilting club, is an important part of the members' lives.

Although most club members are veteran quilters, skill levels can vary considerably, not only because of differences in basic proficiency, but often also because of a variety of age-related physical conditions. As a result, high-quality workmanship, while often evident, is not especially emphasized. Such statements as "We never take out anybody's stitches," and "We can't quilt like we used to, but it don't matter," are frequently heard.[2]

A typical quilting club member (and certainly there are those who do not fit this description) would be a woman over sixty-five who is a longtime resident of Texas and who has never been employed outside her home. She loves quilts, having made and used them all her life, but she probably is not too interested in the state of the art. She would not travel many miles to see a quilt show or attend a workshop. She might greatly admire the specialized techniques currently popular, but she would continue to quilt in the manner she learned as a child. Her participation in a quilting club is not inspired by any conscious desire to see the art survive and evolve. In fact, the history and future of quiltmaking are, as often as not, immaterial to her. The quilt's special significance for the average club member is direct and extremely personal—a significance born of use, familiarity, and memories rather than from some abstract concern about its artistic merits or cultural importance.

As in any organization, the individual member's involvement determines the focus for the group as a whole. So it is that the quilting club's scope tends to be restricted to its own community. There is no need or motivation to seek out similar groups in other areas or to learn new aspects of quiltmaking. The quilting club looks neither outward nor forward. It is static, insular, and, quite simply, complete within itself.

[2]Members of Lytton Springs Quilting Club, interviews with author, Lytton Springs, March, 1979; members of Grace United Methodist Church Quilting Club, interviews with author, Austin, May, 1979.

Traditional quilting clubs exist in great numbers throughout Texas. Almost every community has at least one operating in some fashion, and this will doubtless continue to be the case for several years to come. The set of circumstances that attracted the majority of club members no longer exists, however. On this basis, it is difficult to envision quilting clubs' enduring much longer at current levels.

The quilt guild is based on a different set of circumstances and consequently approaches its subject in a much broader manner. Most guilds are located in cities or else draw together several smaller communities. This wider base results in a much less homogeneous group of participants, who represent a range of ages, skills, races, religions, and economic backgrounds. It also means that most guilds are substantially larger than clubs; some boast two hundred to three hundred members.

This heterogeneous mix makes profiling a "typical" guild member virtually impossible. Guilds currently operating in Texas have members as young as ten and as old as eighty, with the average age being about forty-five. Although guild membership is predominately female, men are welcomed, and a few have joined guilds in larger cities. Depending on the area, anywhere from 10 to 75 percent of a guild's members are employed outside the home, and in the average guild, 45 percent have college educations. Guild members are more likely to have moved to Texas within the last two decades than to be native Texans. Most are not lifelong quilters, and many have become interested in quilts only since the 1970s. Most guild members, however, have good fundamental sewing skills and can readily apply them to basic and specialized quilting techniques. Individual members of a particular guild frequently belong to other guilds as well and may also hold membership in a regional organization such as South/Southwest Quilt Association or a national group like the National Quilter's Association. Through information provided by quilt books, quilt magazines, and organizations they belong to—coupled with visits to shows, festivals, and workshops—the average guild member's knowledge of quilting history, current trends, patterns, color usage, and fabrics is extensive.[3]

Customarily, each guild has a stated purpose, which almost always includes the promotion of quilts as an art form and the education of the public in that respect. Education in all matters relating to quilts is actively pursued within the guild as well, with most groups subscribing to quilt-related publications and maintaining well-stocked libraries, in addition to offering workshops, films, and lectures.

The social element, while considerable, is less pronounced than in quilting clubs, and activities are more varied and enterprising. Most guilds sponsor field trips and special classes, conduct fund-raising activities, and participate in community affairs. Guilds are often asked to provide working exhibits at local events like Ranching Heritage Days in Lubbock, the Folklife Festival in San Antonio, or Spindletop Boom Town Days in Beaumont. Through participation in a variety of activities, guilds have established ties with museums, libraries, public television networks, schools (including colleges and universities), and municipal governments all across the state. For many guilds, the culmination of each year's activity is the staging of a quilt show. The show format varies and may include workshops, a bazaar, commercial exhibits, or a quilted fashion show, but always the main attraction is a display of fine quilts. Public response has been extremely positive, and the yearly guild quilt show is becoming an anticipated occasion in several

[3] Author's questionnaire, submitted to all fifteen Texas guilds existing as of August 30, 1982, responses received and tabulated from fourteen guilds.

communities. Such exposure will doubtless continue to change many people's ideas about quilts.

Guild meetings are usually held monthly at a regular time and place and are conducted according to parliamentary procedure, albeit in a relaxed fashion. The agenda ordinarily contains some form of "bring and brag," where members show off finished projects or works-in-progress, followed by a general business meeting. The program is the main event of the meeting and may include a number of activities. Well-known quilt professionals are invited to give talks and workshops in their various areas of expertise. Quilts are displayed, new techniques are introduced and taught, quilt-related books are reviewed, and useful information about materials and methods are exchanged.

Because guilds tend to have relatively large memberships (the average size is ninety-seven members),[4] many have instituted a system of subgroups, known as bees, to provide more frequent contact and more personal interaction. Bees are established according to a variety of factors, including geographic area or members' work schedules, and are usually limited to about twelve people. Patterned after their namesake, bees bring people together to share experience and work on one another's projects. It is in a bee that guild members most often quilt together around a frame and where novices might receive informal instruction from experienced quilters.

Because of their smaller size, bees are much more social in nature than the guild as a whole, and they often provide the foundation for emotional support and friendships that extend far beyond a common interest in quilts. The weekly or biweekly bees are held in members' homes on a rotating basis, and in addition to working on individual projects,

[4] Ibid.

members might conduct mini-workshops for one another, exchange blocks for friendship quilts, go shopping together for fabrics, or conduct guild business. Most guilds that have an active bee system consider it the backbone of the organization. The bees serve as an extremely effective means of communication within the guild and help sustain a high level of interest in guild activities. Even the largest guilds are able to maintain an atmosphere of intimacy, because bees allow everyone an opportunity to be a vital part of the functioning whole.

Formal organization is a major guild component. Ratification of bylaws represents an important legitimizing step for most groups, and nonprofit status is usually established. Some guilds have even incorporated and retain legal counsel. Money collected from dues and fund-raising activities pays for such things as speakers' fees and honorariums, publicity, library acquisitions, newsletter publication and distribution, special events, and general operating costs. Officers are elected for a specified term from a slate of nominees, and standing committees are appointed. An official logo is designed by each group and displayed at guild functions.

The emphasis placed on high-quality workmanship by guilds is at once subtle and overt, with members encouraged both by example and instruction to strive for a high standard of skill. This emphasis is an essential part of the guild approach to quiltmaking as an artistic endeavor. This is not to say that every quilter is considered to be an artist or every quilt a work of art, but rather that good skills are perceived as the foundation for any creative process.

One of the features of the guild "movement" in Texas is that these groups communicate with one another through newsletters. Many groups exchange newsletters with guilds in other states as well. As a result, information is shared on a regular basis, and quilters in the Rio Grande Valley, for example, are very aware of what those in the Panhandle are doing. This interaction with other quilt-related groups is one of the major differences between the quilt guild and the quilting club.

Historically, the basic guild concept is an urban one and dates from the ancient civilizations of Egypt, Greece, and China. The first guilds were associations of tradesmen established to give members more economic influence and political equality. In Europe and England, the Middle Ages saw the rise of powerful craft guilds, which were made up of artisans skilled in a particular craft. The guild provided many benefits to its members and set standards to ensure high-quality workmanship. The quilt guild of today bears little resemblance to medieval craft guilds, but the ideas of organizing around a common activity and promoting a high standard of workmanship among members are tenets derived from those early organizations.

As applied to quilts and quiltmaking, the guild concept has its origins in the eastern United States. The oldest known quilt study group is the Genesee Valley Quilt Association in Rochester, New York. Sponsored by the Rochester Museum of Arts and Sciences, the group was organized in 1936 by Gladys Reid Holton, a teacher, museum curator, and precursor of today's quilt professionals. Ten years before founding the GVQA, she began delivering lectures on quilts throughout the eastern states. She also traveled all over the world studying textile arts as a representative of the International Country Women's Association. The GVQA's founding objective was "for people interested in quilts and quilting to come together for inspiration and sharing of knowledge and experience in quilting." The group, which has remained active since its inception, established the structure and format followed by many guilds today, ratifying bylaws and featuring guest lecturers, discussions of different techniques, and quilt-related field trips. From the beginning, excellence in workmanship was encouraged among members, and several joined the "11 stitches to the inch society"—that is, pledged themselves to extraordinary proficiency—and won prizes in juried shows.[5]

The U.S. Bicentennial celebration provided the main impetus for the current proliferation of guild activity. During that time, quilts and quiltmaking came to be viewed within the larger perspective of national heritage and thus were elevated to an unprecedented level of mass recognition. In a spirit of cultural discovery and advancement, many guilds were started when individuals or casual groups of quilt lovers decided to formalize their activities in honor of the nation's two-hundredth birthday. The first Texas guild was founded in Houston in 1976.

One urban-related aspect of guild activity is its frequent interdependence with commercial enterprise. With one exception, each city or area in Texas that supports a guild also supports one or more quilt shops, and the quilt-shop owner is almost always an active guild member. Quilt shops depend on quilters for their trade, and quilters in turn rely on shops to provide fabrics, formal instruction, quilt appraisal and restoration, publications, and special supplies. Thus, a mutually beneficial relationship exists between a business venture and a noncommercial organization. Nothing like this link has ever existed before in Texas because members of quilting clubs traditionally used recycled materials and received instruction at home. Moreover, until recently, quilt publications or special services and materials were not even available on a mass scale.

[5]Joyce Gross, "Genesee Valley Quilt Club," *Quilter's Journal* 19 (June, 1982): 5, 6.

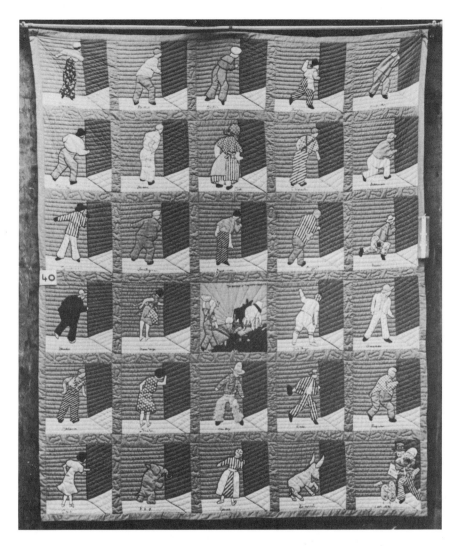

Prosperity, ca. 1930; pieced and appliqué; cotton; 86"x72". Design by Fannie Shaw, Van Alystyne. Photograph from *Quilter's Newsletter Magazine*, issues 73 and 126, by permission of Leman Publications, Inc.

Inspired by Herbert Hoover's Depression-time remark "Prosperity is just around the corner," Mrs. Shaw designed her quilt with all its figures looking for the president's promise. The thirty blocks feature men and women from all walks of life, along with a Republican elephant and a Democrat donkey. In the lower right-hand block Uncle Sam is coming around the corner with bags of money. Mrs. Shaw explained: "I lived what was on that quilt. The footprints that I quilted in the strips between the blocks represent all the steps that people took in all directions huntin' for jobs durin' the Depression."

Bull Durham Tobacco Sack Quilt, ca. 1940; pieced; unbleached domestic, home-dyed; 84″x72″. By Mary Marek, Austin. From the collection of Zoe Williams. Photograph by Jack Puryear.

Women have shown great resourcefulness in their quiltmaking. Both the homemade dyes and the recycled tobacco sacks used in this quilt showed how women could call unexpected things into the service of beauty and warmth.

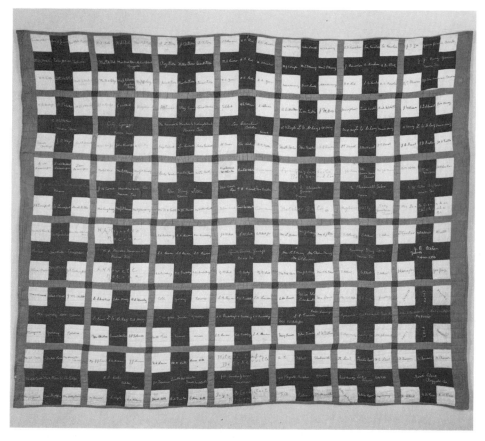

Red Cross Quilt, ca. 1942; pieced signature quilt; cotton. By women of Nocona, Texas. From the collection of Betty Peterson, Austin. Photograph by Jack Puryear.

Signature quilts are usually done as a group gift or commemorative or to raise funds for a charity. When the quilt is done as a fundraiser, each block will typically represent a contribution of a certain amount and will feature a donor's name. On this quilt, for instance, the names of both individuals and firms appear. Both the colors (red, white, and blue) and the pattern suggest the charity for which this quilt was done.

Historic U.S.A., 1936; pieced and appliqué with embroidery; cotton; 93"x-75". By Charles and Fanny Norman. From the collection of Artie Fultz Davis. On display at the Star of the Republic Museum, Washington, Texas.

Also known as the Presidents Quilt, this piece depicts the signing of the Declaration of Independence. It has been exhibited throughout the United States.

Quilt guilds seem destined to define the future of quilts and quiltmaking in Texas. With their comprehensive emphasis and active promotion directed at the general public, guilds will likely do much to eliminate the quilt's musty image and ensure the quilt new status and recognition as a progressing art form. It remains to be seen whether they will also eliminate any "Texan" distinctiveness there may have been in quiltmaking.

The number of guilds in Texas is growing rapidly. Four existed in 1979; by 1982 that figure had almost quadrupled. As interest in quilts continues to expand, indications are that there will be a corresponding growth in guild activity throughout the decade. The following is a list of guilds active in Texas in 1984:

1. Austin Area Quilt Guild
   807 W. 31st Street
   Austin, Texas 78705

2. Bluebonnet Area Quilt Guild
   #59 FM 1456
   Bellville, Texas 77418

3. Central Texas Quilt Guild
   P.O. Box 475
   Austin, Texas 78767

4. Golden Triangle Quilt Guild
   Route 3, P.O. Box 1185
   Kountze, Texas 77625

5. Greater San Antonio Quilt Guild, Inc.
   10910 Lands Run
   San Antonio, Texas 78230

6. Kingwood Quilt Guild
   2070 Little Cedar Drive
   Kingwood, Texas 77339

7. Medina County Quilters' Guild
   Star Route, Box 3AB
   Castroville, Texas 78009

8. New Braunfels Area Quilt Guild
   1244 Fredericksburg Avenue
   New Braunfels, Texas 78130

9. Quilt Guild of Greater Houston
   P.O. Box 79035
   Memorial Park Station
   Houston, Texas 77024

10. Quilters' Guild of Dallas
    15775 N. Hillcrest Road
    Suite 508, Box 304
    Dallas, Texas 75248

11. Quilters' Guild of East Texas
    111 Samuel Street
    Tyler, Texas 75701

12. Rio Grande Valley Quilt Guild
    1901 2nd
    McAllen, Texas 78501

13. South Plains Quilters' Guild
    5403 15th Street
    Lubbock, Texas 79416

14. Trinity Valley Quilters' Guild
    2509 Willing Avenue
    Fort Worth, Texas 76110

15. Val Verde Heritage Quilters' Guild
    404 East 1st Street
    Del Rio, Texas 78840

In 1979, formalized quilt-related activity was extended even further with the establishment of the South/Southwest Quilt Association. The group was co-founded by Karey Bresenhan, who also helped establish the Quilt Guild of Greater Houston and who produces the Houston Quilt Festival each year. Dedicated to "the preservation of fine quilts and the art of quilting," the regional organization sponsors a variety of exhibits, workshops, and activities. The group is based in Houston, but its membership is drawn from across the southern and southwestern United States. With its dynamic and innovative leadership, the organization sets the pace for like-minded groups throughout North America. One of the South/Southwest Association's primary interests is the conservation of old quilts, and the group has developed a plan to sponsor formal training in antique quilt restoration. In collaboration with Vermont's Shelburne Museum, which is noted for textile restoration, the association hopes to develop a corps of well-trained people who will be able to assist museums and other collectors in caring for their quilt collections.

One of the most significant effects of the guild movement is its stimulation of the development of talent. Guild activities also create a framework for showcasing that talent and this, coupled with the quilt's current popularity, contributes to the increasing recognition of singular ability. Certainly this is the case in Texas, where a number of individuals are becoming nationally known for their achievements. Included in this group are not only quilt artists but also pattern designers, innovative quilt-shop owners and entrepreneurs, writers, guild organizers, and teachers.

All of these people are helping to reclaim the quilt from obscurity. With its usage long established, its cultural significance emerging, and its comeback in full swing, the quilt seems to have a secure future in Texas.

CHAPTER 5

Quilts in Texas Museums

The following is a list of Texas museums that have quilts. Not all of the quilts in these collections were made in the state; some were brought from other places by pioneers. Every collection listed, however, does contain some Texas quilts.

Because of the difficulties involved in displaying textiles, some museums, particularly those with large collections, do not keep their quilts on permanent display. Visitors to these museums should encourage the curators to exhibit their quilts as often as possible. Quilts are an important part of our heritage, and they should be seen.

Several museums with fewer than five quilts are listed because their holdings include at least one quilt of particular historical interest; these museums are indicated by an asterisk. All other collections shown comprise five or more quilts. The museums are listed alphabetically by region and city.

Central

1. Daughters of the Republic of Texas Museum
   2nd Floor—Old Land Office Building
   112 East Eleventh
   Austin, Texas 78701
   Telephone: (512) 477-1822

Nine quilts dating from the period of the colonization of Texas, the Texas Revolution, and the days of the Republic of

Texas. One quilt, dated 1829, belonged to members of the "Old Three Hundred," Stephen F. Austin's pioneer colony. The quilts exhibit interesting fabrics and fine quilting. All are on permanent display in glass cases in a historic building located on the state capitol grounds.

2. Texas Memorial Museum
   University of Texas at Austin
   2400 Trinity
   Austin, Texas 78705
   Telephone: (512) 471-1604

Fifteen quilts, none of which are on permanent display. Most of the quilts in the collection are mid-nineteenth century, with one dated 1814. The collection includes a Travis County World War II Veteran Memorial Quilt and a silk doll's quilt. Those interested in viewing the collection should make an appointment two weeks in advance with the registrar of the museum.

3. Bastrop County Historical Society
   702 Main Street
   Bastrop, Texas 78602
   Telephone: (512) 321-6177

A small collection of quilts on permanent display in a historic house. The collection features a tobacco sack quilt.

4. DeWitt County Historical Museum
   312 E. Broadway
   Cuero, Texas 77954
   Telephone: (512) 275-6322

A small collection of quilts housed in a historic house. Most of these nineteenth-century quilts are not on permanent display, but an appointment to view the entire collection can be made by calling the museum.

*5. Lyndon B. Johnson National Historic Site
   Johnson City, Texas 78636
   Telephone: (512) 868-7128
Appliquéd quilt (ca. 1850–60), original design, made by Mrs. George Washington Baines, great-grandmother of President Lyndon Baines Johnson, on permanent display at his boyhood home.

6. Henkel Square
   Round Top, Texas 78954
   Telephone: (409) 249-3308
A good collection of quilts on permanent display in a number of historic buildings. Henkel Square is an authentic restoration of Anglo-American and German-American nineteenth-century culture.

7. Winedale Historical Center
   Round Top, Texas 78954
   Telephone: (409) 278-3530
Approximately thirty pieced and appliquéd quilts, some of which are on permanent display in historic buildings. Signed quilts include the dates 1820, 1849, 1860, and 1884, with the latest made before World War II. The collection is worth viewing not only for the diversity of both quality and types of quilting but also for the wide variety of old textiles. Arrangements for viewing the entire collection can be made by calling the center. Appointments should be made at least two weeks in advance.

8. Witte Memorial Museum
   3801 Broadway (Brackenridge Park)
   San Antonio, Texas 78209
   Telephone (512) 826-0647
Voluntary donation (adults—50¢; children—25¢). This is

undoubtedly the best collection in the state. Approximately 165 quilts, featuring a rich variety of types, textiles, and workmanship, date from the early nineteenth century to the present. Included in the holdings are a large number of Texas quilts. None of the quilts are on permanent display. Arrangements to view the collection should be made in advance by calling the curator of decorative arts.

9. Texas Museum of History
   1000 Burleson Street
   San Marcos, Texas 78666
   Telephone: (512) 392-4517

Eighteen quilts, most of which are thought to be over one hundred years old. All of the quilts are in storage, but special arrangements can be made to view the collection by calling Col. R. M. Beechinor, Jr.

10. Railroad and Pioneer Museum, Inc.
    710 Jack Baskin Street
    Temple, Texas 76501
    Telephone: (817) 778-6873

A small collection of quilts, not on permanent display. Arrangements can be made to view the quilts by contacting the director in advance.

*11. Museum of the Supreme Lodge of the Slavonic
     Benevolent Order of the State of Texas (SPJST)
     520 North Main
     Temple, Texas 76501
     Telephone: (817) 773-1575

This small group of four quilts is interesting because they were all made by women of Czech descent. One quilt was apparently made in Europe and brought to Texas in 1903. Another quilt, featuring a map of Texas with all its counties, won first prize at the State Fair in 1908 and again in the Centennial year of 1936. The museum also contains a good collection of Czech crocheted and embroidered items.

12. The Anson Jones Home ("Barrington")
    Washington-on-the-Brazos State Historical Park
    Between Brenham and Navasota, off Highway 105
    Washington, Texas 77880
    Telephone: (409) 878-2214

The restored home of the last president of the Republic of Texas contains five quilts, all of which are on permanent display. The collection features a Masonic quilt believed to have been the property of Anson Jones, who obtained the charter for the first Masonic Lodge in Texas in 1835.

13. Star of the Republic Museum
    Washington-on-the-Brazos State Historical Park
    Between Brenham and Navasota, off Highway 105
    Washington, Texas 77880
    Telephone: (409) 878-2461

A good collection of fifteen quilts, most of which are not on permanent display. The collection contains "Historic U.S.A.," a magnificent quilt made in 1936 by Charles and Fanny Normann, which depicts the signing of the American Declaration of Independence and the U.S. presidents through 1936. Arrangements can be made to view the entire collection by calling the museum in advance.

14. Ellis County Museum
    102 South College (on the Square)
    Waxahachie, Texas 75165
    Telephone: (214) 937-9283

A good collection of approximately fifty quilts, most of which were made in the Ellis County area in the mid-nineteenth century. Several quilts in the collection were made with material that was homegrown, home-carded, homespun, home-dyed, and home-woven. One carriage or lap quilt, done in the crazy pattern of silks, wool, and velvet, was made for a prominent Waxahachie judge at the turn of the century. This quilt was handed down through the firstborn child of succeeding generations, with each owner's name and date of attaining possession embroidered on the quilt. The latest date in evidence is 1946. The quilts are not on permanent display, and arrangements must be made for viewing the collection by contacting the curator.

East

1. Howard-Dickinson House and Depot Museum
   Rusk County Heritage Association
   501 South Main
   Henderson, Texas 75652
   Telephone: (214) 657-2411

Twelve representative nineteenth-century quilts and one child's quilt made in the 1930s. The Howard-Dickinson House also contains a pine quilt chest made in 1804. Arrangements can be made to view the entire collection by calling the Heritage Association.

2. Harris County Heritage Society
   1020 Bagby, Sam Houston Park
   Houston, Texas 77002
   Telephone: (713) 223-8367

A good collection of mostly nineteenth-century quilts, including sixteen pieced quilts (1830 to early 1900s), nine appliqué quilts (1830 to 1900), and twelve crazy quilts and pieced throws (1870 to 1920). Those interested in seeing the entire collection should make an appointment in advance through the society's administrative office.

3. Sam Houston Memorial Museum
   1804 Sam Houston Avenue
   Huntsville, Texas 77340
   Telephone: (409) 295-7824
A small collection of nineteenth-century quilts on permanent display. The museum also contains quilting frames that belonged to Margaret Lea Houston, Sam Houston's wife.

4. Jefferson Historical Museum
   203 West Austin Street
   Jefferson, Texas 75657
   Telephone: (214) 665-2775
Twelve quilts dating from the late nineteenth century and the early 1900s. The collection is on permanent display in a historic building.

5. Fort Bend County Museum
   500 Houston Street
   Richmond, Texas 77469
   Telephone: (713) 342-6478
A collection of seventeen quilts, featuring one made by the Daughters of the Texas Revolution, a pictorial quilt with scenes from Fort Bend County history, and a signature quilt made in 1906 to raise money for the Christian Church in Rosenburg. Some of the quilts are on permanent display, but most are in storage. Arrangements can be made to view the entire collection by contacting the museum in advance. Fort Bend County was settled by members of Stephen F. Austin's colony, and the museum's holdings include artifacts that belonged to Jane Long.

Gulf Coast

1. Texana Museum
   403 North Wells
   Edna, Texas 77957
   Telephone: (512) 782-5431

Some fifteen quilts, which are exhibited several at a time on a rotating basis. Although most of the quilts were made in Jackson County, two were brought to the area from Mississippi, where they had been made by slaves prior to the Civil War. Special group arrangements can be made to view the entire collection by contacting the museum.

2. Rosenberg Library
   2310 Sealy
   Galveston, Texas 77550
   Telephone: (409) 763-8854

Eight quilts, most of which belong to the Morgan family (a prominent old Galveston family) collection, dating from the mid-nineteenth century. None of the quilts are on permanent display, but a special appointment for viewing them may be made by contacting the museum curator.

3. Plantation House Museum
   Varner-Hogg State Historical Park
   FM Road 2852, off Highway 35
   West Columbia, Texas 77486
   Telephone: (409) 345-4656

Quilts from the personal collection of Miss Ima Hogg, including one made in 1876 for the U.S. Centennial and one made of calamanco glazed with beeswax. Many are examples of fine workmanship, and all are in relatively good condition.

North

1. Fire Hall Museum
   116 North Main Street
   Crowell, Texas 79227
   (No telephone)

A small collection of quilts on permanent display in a historic building. One of the museum's quilts is a "suggan," or cowboy's quilt, made of heavy wool.

2. Dallas Historical Society
   Hall of State
   Fair Park
   Dallas, Texas 75226
   Telephone: (214) 421-5136

The Dallas Historical Society's collection of quilts is not on permanent display. Arrangements can be made to view the collection by contacting Kathleen R. Hallock, the associate curator, for an appointment.

3. Wise County Heritage Museum
   1602 South Trinity
   Decatur, Texas 76234
   Telephone: (817) 627-5586

Fifteen quilts on permanent display, housed in the former administration building of Dallas Baptist College (formerly Decatur Baptist College). The collection features a pictorial quilt of the college and a signature quilt made in 1929 to raise money for a school building in the Cottondale community.

*4 Eisenhower Birthplace State Historic Park
   208 East Day
   Denison, Texas 75020
   Telephone: (214) 465-8908

Tumbling Blocks quilt (ca. 1890–1900), made by Ida Eisenhower, mother of President Dwight D. Eisenhower, on permanent display. Her sons are said to have helped their mother cut out the blocks for this quilt.

5. Tarrant County Black Historical Society
    1150 E. Rosedale Blvd.
    Fort Worth, Texas 76104
    Telephone: (817) 332-6049
A small collection of quilts, including a String Quilt and a Britches Quilt, made by black quilters.

6. Morton Museum of Cooke County
    Corner of Dixon and Pecan Streets
    Gainesville, Texas 76240
    Telephone: (817) 668-8900
A collection of twelve quilts, most of which were made in the Gainesville area about the turn of the century. The quilts are not on permanent display, and an appointment to view the collection should be made in advance by calling the museum.

7. Governor Hogg Shrine State Historic Park
    Park Road 45
    Quitman, Texas 75783
    Telephone: (214) 763-2701
A small collection of Governor and Mrs. Hogg's personal quilts. At least one of the quilts on display in the Honeymoon Cottage was made by Mrs. Hogg.

8. Old West Museum
    Sunset, Texas 76270
    Telephone: (817) 872-2027
A small collection of quilts featuring one with a Bull Durham tobacco sack top backed by sugar sacks, which was

made on a Montague County ranch. Arrangements to view the collection can be made by calling the curator in advance.

Panhandle-Plains

1. Panhandle-Plains Historical Museum
   2401 Fourth Avenue
   Canyon, Texas 79016
   Telephone: (806) 655-7194

A good collection of approximately fifty quilts, the majority of which are nineteenth century. As far as could be determined, the Panhandle-Plains Historical Museum owns the oldest quilt in the state, a Tree of Life done in reverse appliqué and dated 1809. The collection also includes a satin autograph quilt done in the late 1930s featuring the signatures of cowboys from the XIT Ranch. None of the quilts are on permanent display. Those interested in viewing the collection should make an appointment in advance by contacting the curator of textiles.

2. Crosby County Pioneer Memorial Museum and
      Community Center
   101 W. Main, on Highway 82
   Crosbyton, Texas 79322
   Telephone: (806) 675-2331

Thirteen quilts and three quilt tops, none of which are on permanent display. The oldest was made in 1820, the most recent in 1922. Arrangements can be made to view the entire collection by contacting the museum in advance.

3. Deaf Smith County Historical Society, Inc.
   400 Samson (across from the courthouse)
   Hereford, Texas 79045
   Telephone: (806) 364-4338

A representative collection of seventeen quilts dating from

the mid-nineteenth century to the 1930s. The collection includes a Pants Leg quilt. Special arrangements to view the quilts can be made by contacting the executive director of the society.

4. The Museum
   Texas Tech University
   4th Street at Indiana
   Lubbock, Texas 79409
   Telephone: (806) 742-2442

This excellent collection of approximately one hundred fifty quilts is one of the finest in the state and features a variety of types, textiles, and workmanship. The quilts are not on permanent display; special arrangements can be made to view the collection by calling the curator of costume and textiles. Appointments should be made at least two weeks in advance.

5. Carson County Square House Museum
   Fifth and Elsie Streets
   Panhandle, Texas 79068
   Telephone: (806) 537-3118

Sixteen quilts, many of which are on permanent display throughout the museum. Most of the quilts were made in the Carson County area; these include a friendship quilt made in 1917 by the Ladies' Aid Society of White Deer and a quilt made by the Panhandle Chapter of the Rainbow Girls. The oldest quilt in the collection is believed to have been made in 1830. Arrangements to view the entire collection can be made by contacting the museum in advance.

6. Ralls Historical Museum
   801 Main Street
   Ralls, Texas 79357
   Telephone: (806) 253-2425

Fifteen quilts on permanent display housed in a two-story landmark building. Most of the quilts are from the Ralls area. Every two years the museum sponsors a quilt show, averaging seventy quilts per show. A quilting club meets at the museum for an all-day bee the second and fourth Tuesday of each month.

West

1. Colorado City Historical Museum
   175 West Third Street (across from City Hall)
   Colorado City, Texas 79512

A small collection of quilts on permanent display. The most recent quilt in the collection is dated 1931. One crazy quilt made in the late 1800s is lined with homespun fabric that was colored with dye made from the hulls of black walnuts.

2. Fort Concho Frontier Fort and Museum
   213 East Avenue D
   San Angelo, Texas 76903
   Telephone: (915) 655-9121, ext. 441

Twenty nineteenth-century quilts, most of which were made by ancestors of San Angelo residents who brought the quilts with them when they moved to the area. Several of the quilts are on permanent display, but most are in storage. Special arrangements can be made to view the entire collection by calling the registrar in advance.

Bibliography

Published Sources

Allen, Winnie, and Carrie Walker Allen. *Pioneering in Texas: True Stories of the Early Days*. Dallas: Southern Publishing Company, 1935.

Beaumont Enterprise-Journal, November 23, 1980, p. 148.

Benberry, Cuesta. "The Twentieth Century's First Quilt Revival." *Quilter's Newsletter Magazine*, July–August, September, October, 1979.

Bray, Rosemary L., and Roland F. Freeman. "Keepsakes." *Essence*, November, 1978, pp. 106–14.

Brown, Dee. *The Gentle Tamers: Women of the Old West*. Boston: Christopher Publishing House, 1940.

Chase, Patti. *The Contemporary Quilt: New American Quilts and Fabric Art*. New York: E. P. Dutton, 1978.

Cooper, Patricia, and Norma Bradley Buferd. *The Quilters*. Garden City, N.Y.: Doubleday & Company, 1977.

Custer, Elizabeth M. *Tenting on the Plains, or General Custer in Kansas and Texas*. New York: C. L. Webster & Company, 1887.

Daugherty, Wilna Morton. *She Did What She Could: History of a Pioneer Woman*. Waco: Texian Press, 1977.

Dubbs, Emanuel. *Pioneer Days in the Southwest, 1850–1879*. Guthrie, Okla.: State Capital Company, 1909.

Edelson, Carol. "Quilting: A History." *Off Our Backs*, May, 1973, pp. 13–14.

Farm Journal and Farmer's Wife, February, 1941, p. 46.

Fehrenbach, T. R. *Lone Star*. New York: MacMillan, 1968.

Finley, Ruth. *Old Patchwork Quilts and the Women Who Made Them*. Philadelphia: Lippincott, 1929.

Flanagan, Sue. *Trailing the Longhorns*. Austin: Madrona Press, 1974.

Glaspell, Susan. "A Jury of Her Peers." In *Literature: Structure, Sound and Sense*, edited by Laurence Perrine. New York: Harcourt Brace Jovanovich, 1978.

Greenberg, Andrea. "American Quilting." *Indiana Folklore* 5, no. 2 (1972): 264–79.

Gross, Joyce. "Genesee Valley Quilt Club." *Quilter's Journal* 19 (June, 1982): 5, 6.

Hall, Carrie A., and Rose G. Kretsinger. *The Romance of the Patchwork Quilt in America*. Caldwell, Idaho: Caxton Printers, 1936.

Hechtlinger, Adelaide. *American Quilts, Quilting and Patchwork*. New York: Galahad Books, 1974.

Hedges, Elaine. "Quilts and Women's Culture." In *In Her Own Image: Women Working in the Arts*, edited by Elaine Hedges and Ingrid Wendt. Old Westbury, N.Y.: Feminist Press, 1980.

Hill, Kate Adele. *Home Builders of West Texas*. San Antonio: Naylor Company, 1938.

Hogan, William Ransom. "Amusements in the Republic of Texas." *Journal of Southern History* 3, no. 4 (November, 1937): 398–99.

Holstein, Jonathan. *American Pieced Quilts*. New York: Viking Press, 1972.

Hunter, Marvin, ed. "Reminiscences of Mrs. J. J. Greenwood." *Frontier Times* 2, no. 3 (December, 1924): 12.

Ice, Joyce, and Judith A. Shulimson. "Beyond the Domestic: Women's Traditional Arts and the Creation of Community." *Southwest Folklore* 3, no. 4 (Fall, 1979): 37–44.

Ickis, Marguerite. *The Standard Book of Quilt Making and Collecting*. New York: Dover Publications, 1959.

Johnson, Vance. *Heaven's Tableland: The Dust Bowl Story*. New York: Farrar, Strauss and Company, 1947.

Langford, Susan Roach. *Patchwork Quilts: Deep South Traditions*. Alexandria, La.: Alexandria Museum, 1980.

Lewis, Willie Newbury. *Between Sun and Sod: An Informal History of the Texas Panhandle*. College Station: Texas A&M University Press, 1976.

Looscan, Mrs. M. "The Women of Pioneer Days in Texas." In *A Comprehensive History of Texas, 1865 to 1897*, edited by D. G. Wooten. Dallas: Wm. G. Scharff, 1898.

McKim, Ruby. *101 Patchwork Patterns*. New York: Dover Publications, 1962.

Mainardi, Patricia. "Quilts: The Great American Art." *Feminist Art Journal* (Winter, 1973): 17–25.

Mason News, December 15, 1888.

Maverick, Mary A. *Memoirs of Mary A. Maverick*. San Antonio: Alamo Printing Company, 1921.

Morrison, Toni. *Song of Solomon*. New York: Alfred A. Knopf, 1977.

Nunn, W. C. "Mary Austin Holley." In *Women of Texas*. Waco: Texian Press, 1972.

Olmsted, Frederick L. *A Journey through Texas; or, A Saddle Trip on the Southwestern Frontier*. New York: Dix, Edwards & Company, 1857.

Orbello, Beverly Ann. *A Texas Quilting Primer*. San Antonio: Corona Publishing Company, 1980.

Pennybacker, Anna J. Hardwicke. *A New History of Texas for Schools*. Tyler, Tex.: Privately printed, 1888.

Peterkin, Julia. "The Quilting." In *Black April*. New York: Grosset and Dunlap, 1927.

Pickrell, Annie Doom. *Pioneer Women in Texas*. Austin: Jenkins Publishing Company, 1970.

Porter, Millie Jones. *Memory Cups of Panhandle Pioneers*. Clarendon, Tex.: Clarendon Press, 1945.

Premium List of the Third Annual Texas State Fair (pamphlet). Copy in Texas State Archives, Austin.

"Reminiscences of C. C. Cox." *Quarterly of the Texas State Historical Association* 6, (July, 1902–April, 1903): 127–28.

Scarborough, Dorothy. *The Wind*. New York: Harper & Brothers, 1925.

Shelton, Emily Jones. "Lizzie E. Johnson: A Cattle Queen of Texas." *Southwestern Historical Quarterly* 50, no. 3 (January, 1947): 361.

Smithwick, Noah. *The Evolution of a State, or Recollections of Old Texas Days*. Austin: Gammel Book Company, 1900.

Sprague, William Forrest. *Women and the West, a Short Social History*. Boston: Christopher Publishing House, 1940.

Steinfeldt, Cecilia. *Early Texas Furniture and Decorative Arts*. San Antonio: Trinity University Press, 1973.

Turner, Martha Anne. "Jane Wilkinson Long." *Women of Texas*. Waco: Texian Press, 1972.

Turner, Tressa. "The Human Comedy in Folk Superstitions." In *Straight Texas*, edited by J. Frank Dobie and Mody C. Boatright. Austin: Steck Company, 1937.

Vlach, John Michael. "Quilting." In *The Afro-American Tradition in Decorative Arts*. Cleveland: Cleveland Museum of Art, 1978.

Walker, Alice. "Everyday Use." In *Black-Eyed Susans*, edited by Mary Helen Washington. Garden City, N.Y.: Doubleday, 1975.

Webster, Marie D. *Quilts: Their Story and How to Make Them*. New York: Doubleday, 1915.

Weidlich, Lorre M., and Susan Roach. "Quilt Making in America: A Selected Bibliography." *Folklore Feminists Communication* 3 (Spring, 1974): 17–28.

Williams, Lorece P. "Country Black." In *The Folklore of Texan Cultures*, edited by Francis C. Abernethy. Austin: Encino Press, 1974.

Wooten, Mattie Lloyd, ed. *Women Tell the Story of the Southwest*. San Antonio: Naylor Company, 1940.

Unpublished Sources

Brooks, Una M. "The Influence of the Pioneer Woman toward a Settled Social Life on the Llano Estacado." Master's thesis, West Texas State University, 1942.

Brown, Mrs. Milton. Letter to author, April 7, 1980.

Embree, Henrietta Bacon. Diary, 1856–61. University of Texas Archives, Austin, Texas.

Embree, Tennie Keys. Journal, 1865–84. University of Texas Archives, Austin, Texas.

Johnson, Mrs. Virgil A. Letter to author, August 30, 1980.

Kopecky, Mrs. Vincent. Letter to author, March 3, 1980.

Tinsley, Esther Fields. Notes on Coe family history. Private collection of Betty Peterson, Austin, Texas.

Wooten, Mattie Lloyd. "The Roles of Pioneer Women in the Texas Frontier Community." Master's thesis, University of Texas, n.d.

Yabsley, Suzanne. "Texas Quilt Guild Questionnaire." 1982.

Index

Ranching Heritage Days, 68
Red Cross, 38
Richmond, Tex., 83
Rio Grande Valley Quilt Guild, 74
Rochester Museum of Arts and Science, 71
Romance of the Patchwork Quilt in America (Hall and Kretsinger), 36
"rooster tail," 38
Rosenberg Library, 84
Round Top, Tex., 50, 79

Saint Emanuel Baptist Church, 56
San Angelo, Tex., 89
San Antonio, Tex., 32, 68, 73, 79
San Antonio Museum Association, 79
San Antonio Quilt Guild, Inc., Greater, 73
San Marcos, Tex., 80
Scarborough, Dorothy, 29
Scribner's, 34
Sears-Roebuck catalogue, 47
Semi-Weekly Farm News, The, 34, 36
senior citizens' quilting clubs, 54–56
Seton, Ernest Thompson, 34
Shelburne Museum, 75
Shell quilting design, 37
Shirttail quilts, 58
Signature quilts, 38, 85
slaves: quilts by, 8, 10, 58, 84
Slavonic Benevolent Order of the State of Texas, Museum of the Supreme Lodge of the, 80
sod houses, 28
South Plains Quilters' Guild, 74
South/Southwest Quilt Association, 67, 75
Spindletop Boom Town Days, 68
Star of Bethlehem quilt pattern, 52
Star of the Republic Museum, 81
State Fair of Dallas, 27, 32. *See also* fairs
Sternes and Foster, 37
Stomach quilts, 58
Stonewall, Tex., 50
Strawn, Bea, 45
String quilt, 59, 86
suggan, 23, 85
Sunset, Tex., 86

superstitions, associated with quilts, 13, 48, 60, 61

Tarrant County Black Historical Society, 86
Taylor Bedding Company, 36, 37
Temple, Tex., 80
Templeton, Loree, 45
Texana Museum, 84
Texas: Observations, Historical, Geographical and Descriptive in a Series of Letters (Holley), 48
Texas Memorial Museum, 78
Texas Museum of History, 80
Texas Ranger quilt pattern, 7
Texas Rangers, 25
Texas Republic quilt pattern, 7
Texas Tears quilt pattern, 7
Texas Tech University: The Museum, 88
Texas Woman's Fair, 27. *See also* fairs
Third Annual Texas State Fair, 26. *See also* fairs
Three Cheers quilt pattern, 38
Tobacco Sack quilts, 46, 78, 86
"toenail hanger," 38
Travis, William Barrett, 10
Tree of Life quilt pattern, 87
Trinity Valley Quilters' Guild, 75
Tumbling Blocks quilt pattern, 50, 86
Tyler, Tex., 74

urbanization: and quilting, 39

Val Verde Heritage Quilters' Guild, 75
Vincent, Alta, 63
Vlach, John, 60

Ward, Myrtle, 51
Washington, Tex., 81
Waxahachie, Tex., 26, 81
Webster, Marie D., 34
West Columbia, Tex., 87
Wilman, Mrs. Odessa, 30
Wind, The (Scarborough), 29
Winedale Historical Center, 50, 79
Wise County Heritage Museum, 85
Woman's Home Companion, 34
women's movement, 40